Please do not remove
cover from book

COUNTRY MATTERS

COUNTRY MATTERS

Jo Northrop

Selected illustrations by Beth Munden

FULCRUM PUBLISHING
GOLDEN, COLORADO

The following essays originally appeared in *Country Living* magazine:
"Child's Play," Preserving the Harvest, Protecting the Land," "Country Comforts,"
"My Favorite Cookware," "Spring Cleaning," "Knee Deep in Summer" and
"October Magic."

Library of Congress Cataloging-in-Publication Data
Northrop, Jo.
   Country matters / Jo Northrop.
       p.   cm.
   ISBN 1-55591-150-1
   1. Country life. 2. Country life—North Carolina. 3. North Carolina—Social
life and customs.   I. Title.
GT3470.N67 1994
307.72'09756—dc20   94-17446
                          CIP

Printed in the United States of America
0 9 8 7 6 5 4 3 2

Fulcrum Publishing
350 Indiana Street, Suite 350
Golden, CO 80401-5093
(800) 992-2908

For Kenneth
In memory of the good times

Table of Contents

Introduction

This book probably began in the imagination of a girl growing up on a North Carolina farm, for as early as it is possible to know such a thing, it was my dream to write books. Yet after graduating from the University of North Carolina at Chapel Hill, where I studied journalism, I was caught up in many things, none of them the business of writing books. All too often in life, certain dreams are put aside while we deal with other things that either are important, or seem to be.

All my life I've had the habit of taking notes, real or mental, and filing them away "for the right time." It was not until the death of my husband, Kenneth, in 1989, that the very real idea of writing this book (and God willing, others) came to be. Everyone who has lost a mate knows that awful feeling of treading water, time moving in slow motion, while you try to get your emotions under control, and push grief aside long enough to catch a glimpse of solid ground. With luck, we stop treading and head for shore. Even then, it took me a while to clarify what I wanted to do, and to "settle" this book in my mind. In time, though, I dusted off my dream, decided the "right time" was now, and got busy.

Country Matters is my attempt to share my experiences, joys and sorrows, laughter and tears with others who believe, or may come to believe, how much the country matters. I have

seen a fair amount of the world, met some interesting people, done interesting things, and loved deeply. This I want to share. I also want to share my two perspectives: that of a very active woman with 20/20 vision; then, after I became legally blind in 1976, that of a visually impaired, and still active, woman. If it is possible that losing one sense, means your others are intensified, then I bring that to some of these pieces. Earlier in my life, details of a countryside were vividly graphic, but since the time of impaired vision, things are clearest in peephole focus, and the rest of the world is a wonderful impressionistic painting. Perhaps this altered reality has given me an inner vision that was not always mine. In any case, it was after 1976 that I began to write a column for *Country Living* magazine, about simple country pleasures. (The country child had taken notes!) A number of those pieces are included here, but only where they enhance the point of the book. I hope they will be like a second sip of good wine.

This book is about the country, the natural world, and how much it has meant—and still means—to me. Fragments from my childhood in the country— the times when my dreams were shaped—swirl together with the memories of so many other country homes.

Since country creatures are very important country matters, they appear here in generous measure—from our first Labrador, Tar, to our entire pack. A long-tailed tabby named Poo threads his way through many years, never missing an opportunity to take to the open road, a predilection met with our determination to keep him from harm's way. Poo was a curmudgeon of the highest order, a warm and loving memory to me. It is safe to say there are "animal tracks" throughout this book.

Nothing helps us put our hands on a place, leave our fingerprints there, like matters of hearth and home. Not many years after Kenneth and I were married, we took on the job/joy of restoring an old stone farmhouse. In doing that, we discovered traces of the people who had loved the place before us—in the date of the construction carved in the chimney, the faintly discernible smell of smoked meat in the attic, a mousehole mended with the top of a tin can, or lemon balm running wild near the stone wall out back. We left our fingerprints there, too; I am certain of that. I

write about homely things, things I love. And some I dislike: spring cleaning. It all adds to the rich mix of time in touch with the land.

Since the days when I went afield with my father, outdoor activities have been an important component of my life; consequently, the sporting life is among these country matters. I tell of a float trip down a great salmon river, describing it with a sense of urgency and from memory—my journal of that special time having been lost. Like any person who loves the outdoors, I want to share it, to touch other human beings in such a way that they will look at sporting life differently. And perhaps even go afield, take up a fly rod, breathe the fine air—while there is time. Just as our dreams are often put aside to gather dust, so we assume there will be time, plenty of time, for things we want to do "someday." There is never enough time for everything, but there must be time for some, and with luck, for many of the things we really want to do.

Finally, there's the matter of the importance of a sense of place. And I do not mean a geographic place. Or even our native place, for often in this fast-moving world, we are separated from that. A sense of place, to me, is being in touch with the natural world, finding health and balance and renewal in nature and the seasons. If we are in a place that we love, where we are comfortable, where we have invested ourselves, so much the better. In this book I hope to share my unique perspective, however it is perceived by the reader, on our vital need for a link with the natural world. To me, it has meant getting better, getting back on track after a traumatic loss of vision. Call it faith and hope, if you will. I only know that *country matters*.

SCENES FROM CHILDHOOD

He filled each box and basket with hard candies, chocolate drops, gummy bears, gumdrops, peppermint sticks, and ribbon candy, as well as walnuts, pecans, almonds, chestnuts, Brazil nuts, and all kinds of fruit—shiny red apples, rough-skinned tangerines, bright oranges and kumquats, and sometimes a pomegranate. No mere stocking could hold such largesse.

Sandspurs, Doodlebugs,
and Free-Fall Recall

The round-faced, three-year-old girl in the photograph wears striped coveralls with brass snaps down the front. Hands jammed in her pockets, she is leaning against a brick wall and smiling the smile of childhood. I remember the day my mother took that picture. It was shortly after we moved to our big, two-story, white farmhouse in Hoke County, North Carolina, and I was playing alone in the backyard. I loved my coveralls, the house that seemed so big to me, and the spacious grounds. The country house had many rooms, a big front porch, a small screened-in back porch, and a long, screened sleeping porch. (Porches that were half enclosed and half screened, where you could sleep on cots on very hot nights, were once common in the South.) I could ride my tricycle on the front porch in good weather, and on the sleeping porch when it was rainy. The house had hidey-holes, dark closets, and doors to hide behind when playing Hide-and-Go-Seek. There was a big pecan tree in the backyard, from which a rope swing hung. I would swing there for hours, where my mother could keep an eye on me from the kitchen.

As a child growing up in the country, I had a special awareness of the land. I grew up in the days when no one locked their doors, not even when going on vacation. We knew everyone in our part of the country; we were dutifully warned by our parents never to get into a car with a stranger, but few strangers came around. I couldn't always have friends over to play because friends often lived quite a few miles away, and special plans had to be made to get together. Later, when I was big enough to ride a bike, I could pedal to a neighboring farm to play with the children there. My mother would tell me what time to be home, and it was up to me to comply with her wishes. I spent a lot of time playing alone because both my sister and brother were older and interested in other things.

I believe that children who grow up in the country learn to amuse themselves and become independent early, and they have more freedom because there are fewer distractions. I remember lying on my belly in a field of grass and watching one patch of ground to see how many insects I could count. Over a period of time, there were red ants, black ants, tiny black beetles, sometimes a slim green worm on a blade of grass, and once in a while the special delight of a ladybug or a grasshopper. Some grasshoppers, when caught, would spit on me.

From going barefoot, I knew where the prickly sandspur plants were thickest. I'd choose another path to wherever I was headed be-

cause pulling a sandspur out of bare feet is painful. I knew that the catbirds nested in the roses that thickly covered a wire fence in the backyard. I knew that I was to stay well back from their nest so that I wouldn't frighten the mother bird. And I was never, never supposed to touch the nest or eggs. It was a sore temptation. Although I would hurry by the catbird's nest, many's the time the nesting mother flew off her nest and sailed toward me, fussing and scolding. I knew where powdery ant hills, like tiny mountains, rose up from the sandy soil. Sometimes I'd accidentally step on an ant hill, and the angry little ants would swarm over my feet and legs. But a country kid knows you just brush them off with your hand.

We had bobwhite quail on our land, and I knew the time of year when they hatched. We'd sit on the porch and watch the beautiful little hen lead her brood across the lawn, the chicks looking like tiny powder puffs. I knew that the guineas made their nests and laid their hard, speckled eggs in the blackberry brambles at the edge of the thicket. If we wanted to gather any of the guinea eggs, they had to be removed from the nest with a long-handled spoon, because the guineas would abandon the nest if they smelled human scent. In spring just before nesting, the male guinea would puff his feathers up and attack anything that annoyed him, including dogs and automobiles. We lost a number of guineas on the road each year when they bowed up and rushed at an oncoming car.

Growing up in the country, I knew when it was time to plant a garden, and begged for permission to plant radishes of my own. They came up quickly, and I loved pulling the pretty red radishes from the ground and taking a bunch to my mother. Summers were hot, and time seemed to be in slow motion. I loved the water, and went swimming in any creek, lake, or pond when allowed. I was a true "water rat."

Because those days were safer, I could walk in the woods by myself at any time of year. I had to tell my mother where I was going, of course, and be home when she told me to. As a kid, I didn't have a watch, but could guess the time by the height of the sun. I knew the best places to pick violets in spring, and where the wild arbutus grew, and where to find deep-green ground moss. I knew that in the fall, our grapes would ripen, and pecans would fall from the trees in our yard. We would leave a bushel basket under a pecan tree, and people who happened by could pick up some of the nuts and put them in the basket. Before long, we'd have a bushelful. Friends came to get pecans before the holidays, and I remember going with my mother to help them fill their baskets. In the winter, we'd sit by the fire and crack the nuts and pick out nutmeats, so there'd be plenty for candy, cakes, and pies and for salted and sugared nuts. I still like plain pecans, right out of the shell.

I loved running barefoot down a freshly plowed furrow at harvest time, and loved seeing a field of cotton when it was ready for picking. I loved riding my bicycle on the sandy road beside our house. But when the sun started down and the bullbats swooped over the lane, I knew it was time to go home. Growing up in the country, with horses and mules in the barn, I knew which ones would kick the stall, and which were gentle. I learned to shuck dry corn but didn't like going into the corn crib because sometimes a black snake, in search of mice, would slither under the pile of corn.

I climbed the oak and sassafras trees in the thicket, and built a playhouse in their shade. I'd push my feet under the sand in a ditch and carefully withdraw them, leaving two little "caves." These were "toad houses." I knew where the wasps made their papery nests under the eaves of the tobacco pack-house. I was wary of the places where rattlesnakes might be. My father told me that the cottonmouth water moccasin favors the shoreline of lake, river, and creek, and that on land you'll rarely see one more than two feet above the level of the water. Of special interest was how the doodlebugs dug their conical houses in the sand. I could make the funny-looking little ant lion come to the surface by blowing in its sandy lair, or by stirring it gently with a straw while chanting, "Doodlebug, doodlebug, your house is on fire!" When the big black and yellow butterflies, and the orange ones, and the little white ones fluttered over the larkspur and yellow daisies that ran wild in the side yard, I'd sit among the flowers and hope for a butterfly to light on my head. None ever did, but when I held a bunch of flowers in my hand, the butterflies would hover over them.

I felt that I knew personally the cardinals, jays, catbirds, and flickers that lived around our house as well as the small woodpeckers that drilled on the pecan trees. I loved the sound of the mockingbird. I knew the sour weed that I could chew, and the tough-stemmed knotweed that had a hard, round root ball like a marble—boys at school used root balls as weapons.

As a child growing up in the country, I knew the bumps and gullies, the trees and shrubs, the woods and wildlife on the land, because I was outside so much, and paying attention to nature in the way that some children do. Even today, when I happen to crush a weed underfoot and catch its smell, or see larkspur blooming, or see people stooping, basket in hand, under a pecan tree, my senses whirl me back to a time and place that was so totally familiar.

Child's Play

Earlier in the day, I heard the faint sound of children playing at the new school down the road. Their lively shouting and laughing is an unmistakable, international sound, and today it stirs childhood memories of my country grammar school and the games we played in the schoolyard.

Many of the games children play are a part of our folk heritage. New games are invented as times change, but some of the old ones remain. Hopscotch, Tag, and Hide-and-Go-Seek come to mind, as well as ball games of all kinds.

Today, manufactured balls and bats are readily available, but there was a time when country kids had to make their own. String or rubber balls were made of a stone center wound with twine or thin strips of inner tubing. Bats were hand turned on a lathe, or carved roughly by hand. If there were too few children for a regulation game of baseball, we would play One-Eyed Cat, a game that requires a batter, catcher, pitcher, and fielders but only one base and home plate. The batter either strikes out (three strikes) or gets a hit. He can be "caught out" or tagged as he runs from home to the base and back. If he is declared out, the player who put him out goes to bat. If he strikes out, he goes to the field, the pitcher becomes the catcher, the catcher goes to bat, and the game resumes. The batter continues as long as he is not put out. The game may no longer be called One-Eyed Cat, but I'll wager that schoolchildren are playing some version of it today.

During recess at most country schools, lively contests of Jacks and Marbles would take place, and the seesaw was usually in motion. We also "jumped the board" (two players were needed), a game that called for placing a long, strong, but flexible plank across a log. To make this simple setup work, we had to position the lumber according to the weight of the jumpers. When we were ready to go, the child on the end that was elevated leaped up and landed on the plank, bringing it down and catapulting the other player in the air. This up-and-down frolicking continued until one of the jumpers missed the board and landed on the ground. Then it was someone else's turn. Though the game sounds dangerous, I don't remember anyone getting hurt (we had a sandy playground), and it certainly was fun.

We also played a wacky form of charades, a very old game called Bum, Bum, Bum. For this bit of nonsense (we didn't keep score), you first divide the gang into two teams. One side decides on an occupation, such as a farmer tossing hay, while the other one lines up and waits. While approaching their opponents, the actors chant, "Bum, bum, bum, here we come, all the way from Washington." The other crew answers, "Where are you from?"

"Pretty-girl station," is the reply.

"What's your occupation?" the opposing team demands. The last retort becomes a signal for the entire team to act out their chosen occupation. What a crazy scene! When someone figures out the answer, the groups swap sides and the guessers become the actors.

One of my favorite schoolyard activities was jumping rope. While two girls turned the old plow line, we hopped to singsong verses until a misstep gave someone else a chance. My favorite old jump-rope ditty:

> *Teddy bear, teddy bear, turn around.*
> *Teddy bear, teddy bear, touch the ground.*
> *Teddy bear, teddy bear, climb the stairs.*
> *Teddy bear, teddy bear, say your prayers.*
> *Teddy bear, teddy bear, switch off the light.*
> *Teddy bear, teddy bear, say "Good night."*

Many other games have been handed down over the years—Red Rover, Crack the Whip, Farmer in the Dell, and Drop the Handkerchief are a few that I recall. It is good to remember these old outdoor games, for they are a colorful part of country lore.

A Carolina Country Christmas

When I was a child, the spicy fragrance of mince pie that mingled with the pungent pine scent of burning fatwood meant things were astir in the kitchen on Christmas morning. Those rich smells floating upstairs, the thump of firewood thrown on the back porch, and the muffled clatter coming from the kitchen sent us children scampering from the warmth of our quilt-covered beds. We hurried by the garlanded banister, dashing across the drafty hall into the living room, where the kindling urged along a gently hissing fire.

On the hearth was a collection of small boxes and baskets set out by each of us on Christmas Eve. Santa Claus had a choice of chimneys at our North Carolina farmhouse, but we knew he always came down the one in the living room, because that's where we had the tree. (Even when Father's preference was favored and the tree was put in the wide hall by the front windows, Santa still came down the living-room chimney.) He filled each box and basket with hard candies, chocolate drops, gummy bears, gumdrops, peppermint sticks, and ribbon candy, as well as walnuts, pecans, almonds, chestnuts, Brazil nuts, and all kinds of fruit—shiny red apples, rough-skinned tangerines, bright oranges and kumquats, and sometimes a pomegranate. No mere stocking could hold such largesse.

The tree was always a big one, often cut in the farm woods, and heavily laden with ornaments, lights, festoons, and tinsel. Around the tree were spread all the longed-for surprises we had put on our lists to Santa. Sometimes the surprises did not live up to our hopes, especially during the war years when materials were scarce, and rubber dolls and metal carousels were not to be found. One of those years I received a note explaining the shortages and the reasons for the gifts I had not requested. Santa's handwriting, I recall, strongly resembled that of my older sister.

After admiring our gifts, we'd hurry to the kitchen where preparations had started very early. In country fashion, we feasted at midday on Christmas, or as soon thereafter as kinfolk and friends could assemble. This meant pies had to be in the oven early, freeing it for the roasting of a fresh ham or beef, or both.

There is something very special about a country kitchen, especially at holiday time. Christmas morning, the bustling about of the cooks, the splendid smells and warmth, and the gaiety made it magical. It was the coziest and best place on earth to be, especially if we had a light snowfall, or, more likely, an ice storm. When that happened, the eaves were fringed with icicles, and all the trees outside glittered in coats of ice. To look out the kitchen window at a huge holly, its dark green leaves and brilliant red berries glazed with ice, and see cardinals darting in and out of it, was to witness the kind of magic we would remember forever.

Not only did activity begin early on Christmas morning, but much happened days, and even weeks, ahead. One big project was baking fruitcakes. This was usually done with a friend or relative to

share the work and fun, and, of course,
the cakes. My job each year was to pick
up pecans from under the trees in the
yard before the squirrels took more
than their fair share. Then I had to
shell the nuts. Halves were saved for
decorating candies and cakes, and for
salting and spicing for snacks; broken
nut meats went into cookies, candies,
and cakes.

Often both light and dark fruitcakes were made. Fruitcake batter, stiff with sticky citron, pecans, cherries, and other fruits, was
mixed in a big bowl and forced into tube pans. Then it was baked,
filling the kitchen and the entire house with a distinctive holiday
aroma. When the cakes were cool, they were set in deep cake tins
with wedges of apple and a generous splash of good brandy or rum.
From time to time, the tins were opened to remove withered apple
wedges and replace them with fresh ones, and the smell that rose
from them was truly heady. After several weeks, the cakes were fully
aged, ripe, moist, and delicious. I do not have the recipe for those rich
cakes, though I wish I did. Like much country cooking, Mother knew
how to do it "by heart." Probably the cakes were never made exactly
the same way twice.

Besides fruitcakes, we often had fresh coconut cake. This was
made a couple of days ahead and refrigerated. Along with shelling
pecans, the dubious pleasure of cracking, removing, and shredding
the coconut fell to me. First, Father hammered a nail or forced an ice

pick into the "eyes" of the coconut, turning each one upside down over a glass in order to collect the milk. Then the rest was up to me. Every time I hear the buzz and whir of the food processor in my kitchen today, the memory of the hammer, the coconut, and the grater springs to mind.

Along with cakes and pies, we also had homemade candies. We made these, too, well ahead of time, and the difficult part was to see that some survived until Christmas. All of this may sound like a lot of food—and a lot of cooking—today, but the country custom was to have plenty of goodies on hand to offer to all the visitors who came by with Yuletide greetings.

Christmas dinner itself was spectacular in scope if not in sophistication, and no one was obliged to eat some of everything. There was variety to please the tastes of the many diners: There was almost always a turkey (sometimes that rare treat, a wild turkey fattened on pine mast, the beechnuts and acorns that fell in the woods) and a pan of yellow-brown cornbread dressing; often there was a roast beef or a fresh roast ham, too. Sometimes there was oyster stew or bisque on the stove for anyone who needed an appetizer, and always there were many dishes of vegetables, fluffy rice and gravy, seasoned rice, homemade cucumber pickles, pickled peaches, and cranberry sauce. Sweet potatoes and Irish potatoes might both be served, and there was a lettuce-covered tray filled with celery, olives, and radishes. On a sideboard stood the cakes, pies, and candies, as well as the traditional bowl of citrusy ambrosia. It was a feast of magnitude.

Today, we may not fill a smokehouse with our roasts, or bake so many big fruitcakes, or "hill" potatoes, or serve such an overwhelming variety of food at one holiday feast. But the essence of a country Christmas remains in recipes handed down, in memories and traditions shared. If there is someone in the kitchen who loves to cook, and family or friends who enjoy good food, there can be a country Christmas anywhere.

Miz Eubanks, Thomas Cat, and the King James Grapes

Our friends all knew when the grapes were ripe. Nobody had to ask or telephone ahead. When the sunlight turned that soft gold peculiar to early autumn, friends and neighbors would appear with a bucket or a basket to share in our crop of scuppernongs and King James grapes in our backyard. The vines weren't all that vast, but they were prolific every other year, in the manner of some crops. Bumper crop or slim pickings, there was always enough to share for jams and jellies, preserves, and maybe even a little homemade wine.

Many people in the area had that sweet southern grape, the scuppernong. When ripe, the hull turns a lustrous bronze color, and after a rain, the heady, tantalizing, distinctive sweet smell of ripe scuppernongs would fill the air. Scuppernongs are wonderful for a pinkish jelly and dessert wine. One of my aunts also used to make scuppernong pie, unbelievably delicious.

Good as the scuppernongs were, the real attraction was the arbor of King James grapes. These grapes were a deep, almost black purple. They grew in tight, fat bunches and their skins were tough, so they were easy to pick. At once tart and sweet, the King James grapes were prized for their excellence in preserves, jellies and jams, and again, wine. The pickers did not always admit they were going to make a little wine, but I am sure that grape vine supplied many a bracing nip through the long winter. It was a rare autumn when we didn't have a jug or two gurgling in the corner. The resulting wine was very sweet, but mighty good. My mother made both jelly and grape-hull preserves, a family favorite. The King James grapes had a high sugar content and lots of natural pectin, so it was hard to fail in the jams and jellies enterprise. That was one reason our grapes were so popular. Besides their excellent preserving qualities, both the King James variety and the scuppernongs were fine "table grapes," that is, good for eating right off the vine.

One of our neighbors who always came to pick a few grapes was my mother's good friend, Miz Eubanks— "Mack." Miz Eubanks was a very pretty woman, with soft wavy hair and expressive dark eyes. She was always immaculately turned out, no matter what time of day. When the grapes were ripe, Miz Eubanks would drive up and come in and chat with my mother before repairing to the vine.

She would be wearing a spotless and invariably pretty print cotton dress, and often, red shoes. Miz Eubanks loved red shoes, and they were a sort of trademark of hers. Since a grape picker had to go under the arbor, Miz Eubanks would usually bring a straw hat to protect her hair from the tendrils of the vine and any dusty fallout.

Miz Eubanks was an energetic person, and this energy sometimes manifested itself in a slight nervousness. She was, quite sensibly, afraid of snakes, and being a good country woman, she knew that certain varieties of snakes liked to crawl up into grape arbors and rest in a perfect, leafy bower on warm autumn days. No reasonable person would like to have a snake among her curly locks, no matter how harmless the snake, so Miz Eubanks's straw hat was a carefully considered, reasonable precaution.

One fine autumn day, Miz Eubanks came to pick grapes. "Hey, Mack!" my mother hallooed. "Come on in for a cup of coffee before you start picking." Mack and Margaret sat a spell, rocked, chatted about children, community happenings, and the size of the grape crop this year. Pretty soon the amenities were satisfactorily concluded: Ma went back to her chores and Miz Eubanks tied on her straw hat and went, bucket in hand, to the grapevine down in the backyard. With some apparent trepidation, she squared her hat and ducked under the arbor to fill her bucket with bunches of the sweet grapes.

Now, it is unfortunate that, of all people, it should be Miz Eubanks who picked grapes on the very same day that Thomas Cat, a lanky tabby cat, should be napping among the leafy coolness of the arbor. Thomas Cat had appeared at our back door one day, a big-eyed kitten with a mighty meow. We took him in, of course. My father's name was Thomas, and since this was a little tomcat, I named him

Thomas Cat, after my father, with the peculiar logic of a child. Thomas Cat and I were the best of friends in that special way that only a child and an animal can be. (If we are lucky, we retain that special ability as adults.) Thomas Cat grew to be a fearsome mouser, moderate traveler, and a loyal member of our family. I told him my troubles, and he listened patiently. I laughed, and he'd stretch and roll over, inviting me to scratch his belly. At the first touch, quick as lightning, he'd clutch my hand in all four paws in a mock fight, and pretend to bite it. That meant he was happy, too.

Thomas Cat was nobody's fool. He knew when and where to hunt and which chair had the softest cushion, and he always could charm my mother out of a tidbit when she was cooking fish for dinner. He knew to climb a tree if strange dogs were in the yard, and magically, he always seemed to know where I was. And Thomas Cat was funny and very playful—almost as though he had a sense of humor.

When Miz Eubanks started reaching up into the vines plucking bunches of grapes, Thomas Cat watched with growing interest. As her hands darted in and out, he must have decided this was some kind of game designed especially for his amusement. The cat watched her and waited until her straw hat was directly under him, and then he reached down with one paw, and gave the hat a mighty swat. For good measure, in the stunned millisecond between cause and effect, he reached down (with a paw resembling a striped snake, we can imagine) and gave the bonnet another good shot.

The result was electric. There was a shriek fit to rend the air to Quewhiffle Township, and the fastest retreat I've ever seen. Miz

Eubanks's shoes were a red blur as she thundered up the path, shouting "Snake!" Her straw hat was knocked off and the half-filled bucket summarily abandoned at the arbor.

Well, to cut it short, when Miz Eubanks calmed down and realized she was not snake bit, she and my mother made a cautious inspection of the arbor. They armed themselves with garden hoes before facing the "snake in the arbor." Naturally, they discovered Thomas Cat, full of mischief, curled up and waiting for another "victim."

Miz Eubanks had a wonderful sense of humor, so she appreciated the joke on herself more than anybody. There was unbounded laughter for a while, then great high glee and sporadic chuckling as Mack and my mother filled the bucket with King James grapes. When they came up the path to the house, they were still laughing, the bucket was full—and behind them trailed Thomas Cat.

Preserving the Harvest,
Protecting the Land

Hardly a leaf stirs on this still, sultry July afternoon. Even the birds seem to have taken refuge from the penetrating heat. And most people have gone inside to seek shelter.

In the cool of my kitchen, a basket of summer vegetables stands on the counter, paying tribute to the wonders of the land. Heaped in a beautiful hodgepodge are deep-red tomatoes, bumpy cucumbers, sleek zucchini, yellow crookneck squash, bell-shaped green peppers, crimson chilies, purple eggplant, a scattering of green beans, and a half-dozen ears of young corn, still bewhiskered and in pale yellow-green chunks.

I rinse the vegetables with cool water and set them aside to drain. The eggplant is destined for parmigiana, to be frozen, along with a portion of the beans, for use at a later date. I'll put the corn and tomatoes on the table tonight, string the red chilies to dry, and gradually use up the rest of the produce.

Now I turn to the more time-consuming but pleasant job of peeling peaches. At the farmers' market, I bought a sizable basket of this perfect, ruby-cheeked fruit. I plan to make chutney and pickled peaches, saving plenty for eating out of hand and for cobbler. I select the softer fruit for the gingery, clove-and-cinnamon-spiced condiment and set aside the firmer examples for pickling.

While preparing the fruit, I recall my childhood days when a peach orchard bordered our farmhouse. On a hot evening when the harvest was ripe, we filled an ice-cream container with cream, eggs, crushed fresh peaches, and sugar. We lowered the full container into an old-time, hand-cranked freezer and packed ice and ice-cream salt around it. Next, we threw a burlap bag over the receptacle, and all hands took a turn at cranking. As the ice cream hardened, the handle became tougher to turn, so we assigned a child the job of sitting atop the contraption to weigh it down. To anyone who has never tasted homemade peach ice cream, let me say, simply, that it is a summer pleasure I strongly recommend.

Recovering from my daydreaming, I drop whole, peeled peaches into a bowl of water to which I've added a splash of lemon juice, to prevent the fruit from darkening before all the peaches are processed and sealed in jars. Then, I continue my happy woolgathering about bygone midsummer days.

Sometimes after a scorcher of a day, Pa would take me fishing. As a child, perhaps you noticed how interminably long it took adults to get ready for this activity: "It's too hot to go so early," Pa would tell me when asked if he were ready to leave. "We have plenty of time before sundown," he'd add, tinkering in his metal tackle box, as I watched from my swing under the pecan tree.

Finally, we'd be on our way, driving along with the car windows down, admiring the crops as we followed narrow country roads. An old mill pond, where we fished only a couple of times, became one of my favorite destinations. Hauntingly serene and located in the lower part of the county, the pond was black and still, its surface broken here and there by rings where fish surfaced. We fished from a pirogue-type boat that heeled thrillingly from side to side, nearly swamping whenever we cast our lines. I did more paddling than casting, fearing we'd see a water moccasin as we wended our way among the moss-draped trees standing in the murky water. As the birds cried and the shadows deepened, the evening air became blessedly cooler. We'd quit fishing and tie up the pirogue just as the bullfrogs began croaking and the mosquitoes whining.

Many of us share similar remembrances about activities that are just as pleasurable today. A drive in the country, picking peaches, and going fishing endure, but some things have changed in our land. Like others, I am concerned about the pollution of air and water, the desecration of wetlands and forest lands, and the critical consequences of our carelessness.

I am concerned not only for our country but for the world. We need to cooperate in any way we can to protect our beautiful planet. Caring in small ways counts. I cheer the volunteers who maintain a stretch of highway or byway, picking up the assorted refuse tossed out by motorists and passersby, and I am encouraged by legislation addressing the disposal of solid wastes and other environmental problems. I cherish our simple country pleasures and want future generations to be ale to enjoy them.

I hope there will always be a "fishing hole" with healthy fish to catch, fresh air to breathe, pure water to drink, and wildlife to enjoy. As I bite thoughtfully into a fat, fuzzy peach, I recall a verse from "Yankee Doodle":

And there we saw a thousand men,
As rich as Squire David;
And what they wasted ev'ry day
I wish it could be sav'ed.

When we drove into the yard of the handsome country estate, the owners had the mother of the pups and the entire litter out on the front lawn. What a sight! A light breeze was stirring, and the mother of the litter sat calmly on the perfectly tended lawn, lifting her head and ignoring the yellow and black puppies that waddled all around her on the green grass. When the four of us got out of the station wagon, the Snows came down the lawn to greet us. We hurried over to the puppies. The big female stood, facing us, ready to protect her litter from strangers. She did not growl, but she was watchful. Her owners calmed her so we could approach. Kenneth stooped down and immediately picked up the biggest yellow puppy.

Poo

When Kenneth and I were married, it was understood that Poo and I were a package deal. Poo was fourteen pounds of muscle and sass in the form of a long-tailed, orange tabby tomcat. Poo and I had become allies in this unpredictable world, and I was sure my friendly country cat would get used to a city apartment. We had spent several years together. During that time Poo had been repaired after encounters with other tomcats, a groundhog, and a milk truck. He had overcome acrophobia after climbing up a telephone pole, and had survived being thrown into the cove behind my house by three boys to whom I had given permission to fish from my dock. (The boys did not escape my wrath.)

I got Poo when he was a kitten from my friend Dianne, who had a prolific spotted female that was "Mother Cat" personified. Every time her cat had a litter, Di asked me to take one of the kittens. I kept saying no, but Dianne did not let up. Since her cat always seemed to have batches of black and multicolored kittens, it seemed a safe bet when I promised to take a kitten if the mother "ever had a husky, orange tabby male." One litter later I received a gleeful call from Dianne. "Want to come see your new kitten?" she laughed wickedly.

"You can pick him up in about six weeks." "It's time you had that fecund female spayed," I grumbled.

There was no resisting that feisty pudgy kitten. When I took him home inside my jacket and set him down on the kitchen floor, he streaked through the house, climbed a towel in the bathroom, and sat atop the towel rack like a little orange bird surveying its scary new world. Poo grew to be a handsome cat, with a broad head framed by leg-of-mutton sideburns. The deep orange of his stripes was accented with a white vest and underbelly. He was sociable, and a fearless and agile climber. More than once he seemed bent on proving the theory that curiosity kills a cat. Poo and I were steadfast friends, but when he came to live with Kenneth and me in our New York City apartment, the cat and Kenneth kept a wary distance. "If you'll just talk to him," I told Kenneth, "he'll warm up to you." "I'm not sure I want him to warm up to me. I've seen his teeth when he yawns. And he's scratching hell out of the wing chairs." I knew Kenneth and the big tabby had struck a truce when I saw them napping on the same sofa.

Poo spent a lot of time on the window sills, eye to eye with a constant parade of frowsy pigeons. It didn't take him long to figure out that swatting the windowpanes was a waste of time. Thereafter he just glowered at the preening, noisy birds.

Just when Poo had established his apartment kingdom and his routine, it was invaded by a black Labrador retriever, "Blackmore's Tarheel." Poo distrusted Tar, who was energetic, clumsy, and boisterously friendly. When Tar went tearing in the cat's direction, Poo arched his back, hissed and—thinking better of it—shot to the top of the highboy. He'd crouch there, growling softly at the intruder. Tar would bark excitedly. "The neighbors are going to love this development," Kenneth sighed, picking the puppy up and shushing him. But cats and dogs who share the same home do get along, and after a few skirmishes in which ground rules were established, the tabby and the Lab got along fine. As Tar grew, they'd play together. The cat would be snoozing, minding his own business, and the half-grown dog would nudge Poo with his muzzle, then run away a short distance. He'd come back and nudge the cat again until Poo would leap toward the dog—and the race was on. They ran a circuit: living room, dining room, kitchen, front hall, back to the living room. Racing the course, they'd overturn the water dish in the kitchen, rumple the oriental rug in the hall, and skid into the living room furniture. They'd regain stride, and keep going. Sometimes, as if by a signal, they'd change directions and the dog would pursue the cat. Poo often initiated the game. He would crouch on a table or chest, and when Tar walked by, the cat would ambush him. He'd bound off the dog's back, and the chase would be on again. As long as Poo lived, he and Tar would play together. Never with the Labs that were added to our tribe—only with Tar. People who saw the Lab and the tomcat playing could hardly believe their eyes.

While living in the city we longed for country weekends, and went through a series of rented places. Eventually, we bought a 1795 stone farmhouse near Warwick, New York. Our plan was to go to the country on weekends and, in time, restore the house and move there permanently. We enjoyed the pleasures and advantages of the city, but Kenneth and I both needed time in the country for our personal tranquility and perspective. The old house was very livable as it was, but there were changes we wanted to make to restore its original character. Warwick was a pretty town dating from Revolutionary times. The rolling hill country with its apple orchards, dairy farms, handsome old homes, and small homesteads was very appealing. Kenneth was a member of a sportsmen's club nearby, and there were intriguing countryside antiques shops that I wanted to explore, so it seemed perfect to both of us. Kenneth could train Tar to flush pheasants at his club, and I could putter around the house and prowl in the antiques shops. Poo was the only member of the family who dreaded trips to our country place. He liked mousing and exploring in the old house, but it was getting there that was the problem. Poo suffered awfully from motion sickness. Just going up or down in the elevator in our building caused him to be rather spectacularly ill. I disliked leaving him alone in the city apartment over a weekend, but I hated to subject him to the one-and-a-half-hour ride to the country. He didn't do well traveling over perfectly flat terrain, and the route to Warwick was very hilly. I consulted our veterinarian. He suggested we give Poo a pill for motion sickness before we left town on Friday afternoon. It was worth a try, but I'd had unsuccessful bouts of trying to give Poo medicine.

When Poo saw me with a pill bottle in my hand, he raced for our bedroom closet, leaped to the top shelf, and burrowed under a pile of sweaters. I found him, plucked him off the shelf, and carried him into the living room, where I sat with him on my lap. With the pill concealed in a small meatball, I offered it to the wary cat. Poo would have none of it. He sniffed the little meatball suspiciously and tried to jump off my lap. I used all the tricks the vet had shown me. No luck. Poo was gentle, but purveyors of medicine could come out the worse for wear. I crushed the pill and scattered the powder on his favorite food. He wouldn't touch it. Kenneth tried to give the crusty kitty the pill and gave up after round one. I continued to put the pulverized pill in his food each Friday, hoping he'd get enough medication to soothe him on the trip to the country. Once in a while he might take a nibble, but would taste the medicine immediately, and eat no more.

After a few miserable trips with the cat, we consulted the vet again, this time about the wisdom of leaving the cat in the apartment over the weekend. The vet told us that if we left plenty of dry food and fresh water, the cat should be perfectly all right for such a short time. This worked well until we came home from the country one Monday morning and found Poo listless, panting, and constantly getting in and out of the litter box. I called the vet immediately, and was told to bring Poo to his office as fast as I could. The office was a few blocks away, and I could make it faster on foot than in a cab in the heavy traffic. So I put the sick cat on a small blanket in his travel case, and hurried off. When the elevator doors opened on the first floor of our building, I ran across the lobby, zoomed past the astonished doormen, and ran as fast as I could to the vet's office, dodging people on the sidewalk in my headlong rush. Poo was too sick to complain about the bumpy ride. I rushed into the back where the doctor was waiting. Poo had been altered, and the vet told me that male cats who have had this procedure are subject to cystitis. This was Poo's case, and for the first time, he could not relieve himself. He had to be catheterized, and was given an injection. A minor flood was the happy result, and I was able to take my orange tabby home, with medication (liquid, thank goodness) and instructions. I was warned that this might happen again, but with the medication the possibility would be minimized. Also, I was told that cat food with high ash content was bad for an altered male cat, and the food he had been eating on weekends was dry, for the obvious reason that canned food left in a dish might spoil. When Poo got well, it meant he would either have to stay at a commercial kennel or go with us to Warwick on weekends.

We all dreaded the trips, because we suffered along with Poo. When we started packing a few bags late Friday, Tar, always eager to go, would sit beside the front door so we couldn't leave without him. Poo would disappear. He would hide in the kitchen, under a bed, behind sofa cushions, anywhere he could think of. I'd put a thick stack of newspapers in his carrying case, and the moment I placed him in the case on the papers, he'd begin to complain. It was heart rending, but he had to go with us. His first accident would take place in the elevator. So I'd dispose of the top pieces of newspaper before we even got into the station wagon. At first we placed Poo on the backseat (still in his case) with Tar, but the second the cat started to heave and yowl in misery, Tar would leap into the front seat between Kenneth and me. After several crowded trips, I finally gave in and let the dog have the front seat, and I sat in back with the miserable cat. We'd make several stops along the way to dispose of used newspaper. For obvious reasons, we had to leave a window partially open, even in the middle of winter. After the first half hour, the cat would adjust to the motion of the station wagon, and would settle down for a nap. When we arrived at the farm, we'd open his case and he'd jump out, spry as a kitten. But that first half hour of every trip was no fun, especially for Poo. When finally we restored the old farmhouse and moved there full time, I'm sure Poo would have voiced his approval, had he been able to talk.

It was quite some time before we were able to make the big move to the country. Meanwhile, Poo, who once had plenty of out-door freedom, never missed a chance to get out of the apartment and have a look at the city. I had little signs on the front door, inside and out, warning guests not to let the cat out. But when the service bell rang at the back door at the end of the kitchen, Poo would race there and jump up on a counter; the moment the door was opened, the cat was an orange streak springing past a startled delivery man. There was no way Poo could go except down the six flights of stairs. So I'd buzz the custodian and warn him that my orange tabby was on his way downstairs, and would ask him to watch out for the cat. I'd hurry downstairs and collect the escapee from the custodian. When I first saw Poo's aerial escape act, I prepared my defense for the next time the bell rang. When that day came, and I hurried to the back door and opened it, I whirled around in order to catch Poo in midflight; I was chagrined to see a streak of orange instead speed around the feet of the delivery man and disappear down the stairs. "Put the package on the counter," I said, frantically cramming a tip into the man's hand. Politeness, shock, amusement, and acceptance that he had met a true mad woman ran over his face like the pictures in a slot machine. I raced over to the intercom. "What was that orange thing?" he asked, pocketing the money. "My cat," I said, impatiently punching the buzzer on the intercom. "Big 'un," he said. "He'da made a helluva quarterback." I nodded agreement and he closed the door. I could hear his laughter trailing down the stairs.

"Halloo, Mrs. Narthrap, and what'll ye be needing this fine marning?" asked Mr. Kelly, the custodian, in his usual ebullient Irish way.

"My cat's coming down the back stairs again, Mr. Kelly. Catch him, and I'll be right down."

"Ah, the rascal has gone streaking again, has he?" Mr. Kelly singsonged. "Never you mind, I'll catch 'im as sure as me name is Kelly."

"Thank you, Mr. Kelly." Mr. Kelly was so cheerful about cornering my cat, I wondered if he might have had a wee cup of Irish coffee at morning. When I went out the back door to retrieve my wanderlusty feline, I heard a row several landings down. I ran down and found Mr. Kelly and the delivery man doing their best to hold Poo between them. The big cat did not want to be held, that was clear. Mr. Kelly was trying sweet persuasion. "There now, laddie," he cooed, trying to stroke the struggling cat. The problem was, Poo stroked back, giving Mr. Kelly a quick cuff. "Yow!" Mr. Kelly hollered, holding his scratched hand, and letting out a stream of words that I suspect were Gaelic expletives. The delivery man's cap had fallen off, his face was flushed, but he held the caterwauling cat at arm's length, thrusting him in my direction. I took Poo in my arms, admonishing him. "*Riaow!*" was Poo's parting shot.

I apologized profusely to Mr. Kelly, who had quieted down and assumed his usual pleasant demeanor. "That's a tough kitty you have there, Mrs. Narthrap. I never had a minute's trouble with the lad before."

"What happened?" I asked. The cat had the effrontery to settle comfortably against my chest, staring distrustfully at the two men, while purring loudly. "I'm so sorry," I said. "What happened?"

The delivery man stooped to pick up his cap. He brushed his disheveled hair with his hand and put his cap on. "I overtook the big streaker on the second floor landing. He'd stopped to see if he could open the metal door there. He was pulling at it with his claws. Locked, of course. Just as he looked up, I tried to grab him. He spat at me, gave me a nip, and, starting down to the first floor, he bumped into Mr. Kelly, who was coming up the stairs. On the third floor we cornered him on the landing. But only because he had stopped to try that door, too. You saw the rest."

"I really am sorry," I repeated. "I'll be glad to put something on your scratches."

They both refused, laughing. "No," said Mr. Kelly, "we have cats, too. I'm used to it."

The delivery man looked at Poo, now as calm as a kitten after a bowl of cream. "I've changed my mind," he said. He pointed at the cat (at a safe distance, I noticed). "You would make a hell of a fighter. Be in contention your first year." He grinned. "I'll be on the lookout for him the next time I have to make a delivery at your place."

"Thank you, both of you," I said. I climbed the stairs to our back door, which was still ajar. Poo was no longer purring, but was slowly switching his long tail to and fro. I stepped into the kitchen and kicked the door shut. Tar was waiting, wagging his tail, wanting to see what all the excitement was about. Poo jumped out of my arms and over the dog. He whirled and swatted Tar's tail. The Lab scrambled around and took off after the streaking cat. I turned on the teakettle as the cat and dog ran around the apartment, like a two-figure merry-go-round. I knew how the circling would end. Either Tar would tire of it, take a stand, and growl lightly, signaling that the game was over—or Poo would leap to the top of a chest or other high place and crouch with his feet together and his tail curled around his body. Then he'd close his eyes and ignore Tar, who would soon go off and settle down on a rug for a nap himself. And I could have a quiet cup of tea. It was like a crazy ritual.

Poo was such an escape artist that Kenneth called him "Houdini." "Houdini's" skills reached their peak one summer when we rented a beach house at Quogue, on Long Island. We were fortunate to find a rental place that would permit pets. The owners of the house had a dog themselves, so they had built a fenced-in area adjacent to a utility room and installed a dog door. Their pet could go out and come inside at will. It was the perfect setup for Tar. What we hadn't counted on was Poo's instant cognition of the dog door as a cat door. The door, just big enough to permit a dog's passage, was equipped with stout baffles that were flexible, but required a healthy push before they gave way. Tar would bolt through the baffles. Poo would just squeeze through them, jump the fence, and head for the dunes. We had to keep the utility door shut so Poo wouldn't escape.

We discovered that Poo could get out the second day we were at the beach, when I opened his can of dog food and the sound of the electric can opener did not bring him meowing into the kitchen. (Yes, dog food. Poo ate Mighty Dog because it was ash free and high in protein, just what the vet ordered after the cat's episode of cystitis. We couldn't find a cat food that met our needs—so Mighty Dog it was. Poo took to it as readily as he did to asparagus tips.) When I couldn't find the cat, I went out on the deck where Kenneth was waiting for me to join him. He was in swim trunks. We were planning to walk along the path through the dunes and have a swim in the ocean before dinner.

"What's the matter? Why aren't you in your swimsuit?"

"Poo's gone," I said, trying to hide my alarm. I understood the cat's longing to explore the countryside, but we couldn't let him wander.

"Oh, hell," Kenneth said, rising from the lounge with the resigned air of a man who had faced this problem before. "You listen out back, and I'll walk down the path a way and listen, too." Kenneth set off through the beach grass and I went to the back porch. I whistled. (Besides eating dog food, Poo also responded to a whistle the same way a dog does.) I couldn't hear the bell on his collar. It was a good-sized bell that could be detected from quite a distance. I could hear Kenneth out on the dunes, whistling. This scene  would be repeated many times during the summer, sometimes with Kenneth chasing the cat through the beach grass. An onlooker would not be able to see the cat, only the apparently eccentric man thrashing through the waist-high sea oats. But this time, the cat couldn't be found. We regrouped on the deck.

"He'll be back," Kenneth comforted me. "That cat is smart enough to find his way home." "Come on, let's have a swim. It will do us both good, and I'll wager by the time we get back, Poo will be home. If not, we'll check at every house up and down the beach. He hasn't gone far." I reluctantly agreed, and we set off down the path to the ocean.

After our swim, I grabbed a towel and ran back through the dunes to the house. There was a shower out on the deck, so I stepped under it to rinse off the saltwater. I hurried through the house to the back porch and whistled. I listened. I could hear nothing but the ocean breeze. No tinkling bell. Dejected, I turned to Kenneth. "We'll have to start knocking on doors."

"As soon as I get into dry clothes," he said, heading for the bedroom.

Then, on the wind, there was a hint of a bell. Was I imagining it? "I think I heard Poo!" I shouted, running to the back porch. Sure enough, in the middle of the driveway, here came Poo, his bell jingling with every haughty step. He was carrying a long-tailed mouse.

We had a wonderful summer on Long Island, a truly golden time. Poo must have enjoyed it, too, because he got a lot of exercise scampering through the dune grass. We tried to keep him inside, but with a constant stream of houseguests going in and out, Poo would give us the slip. I will always remember Kenneth, barefoot and in swim trunks, walking from the dunes to the house, with arms outstretched, holding the kicking cat at a safe distance.

The big tabby never had a problem adapting to the changes in our lives. He was a constant mouser at our farmhouse in Warwick. He was choosy about his friends, but when my mother visited us, he would climb in her lap at every opportunity. She stroked him and told him what a handsome old kitty he was, and he ate it up. At that time, we not only had Tar, but three other Labrador retrievers: two blacks, Nikki and Jedediah, and one yellow, Drambuie. Tar, Nikki, Jed, and Buie soon learned to respect the fearless tabby. They'd tease him, but he stood his ground. They never ganged up on him, and after a while, Poo would rub against the Labs, in the subtle way in which cats express friendship. Sometimes he would curl up on a table or counter and when a Lab happened by, Poo would reach down with a paw and give the dog a swat on the back. Never the head. The dogs hardly noticed. It was harmless, and they were used to the cat's shenanigans. Wherever we lived, in wintertime the dogs would sprawl in front of the fireplace, all four of them forming a ragged half moon. As soon as the dogs settled down, just like clockwork Poo would stroll in among them, stepping past legs, muzzles—and over a body if he had to. He was unafraid of the dogs, and they ignored him. Then the cat would stretch out on his side, extending his full length, in the semicircle of dogs—but nearest the fire. Being wise to the adage, "let sleeping dogs lie," I always held my breath when Poo walked over them.

Like all cats, Poo was wary of strange dogs, and he simply would not tolerate other cats. He also disliked noisy gatherings at our house. When too many people created too much noise for him, he'd go to our bedroom and crawl under the bedspread. He'd stay there until everyone left. Poo liked napping on our bed, especially if it was unmade. Often when making the bed, I'd snap a sheet and Poo would go flying through the air like an acrobat. He also liked to curl up in a cheese basket that I kept on a table. It was his favorite basket, and it was barely big enough to hold his body. But he'd curl up inside it with his head almost tucked under his rear end. He looked like a fur pillow idly placed in a basket. He liked hidey holes, high places, napping near a window, the top of the refrigerator, walking narrow rails, rooftops, and open suitcases. He would, if you didn't watch out, fetch a houseguest's socks or underpants into the living room for everyone's inspection. Maybe he hung round the retrievers too much. They were a band of notorious pursesnatchers, but Poo never took up that pastime.

Poo seemed to know when anyone "had the blues." If you were sad or "stressed out," Poo would stick to you like peanut butter. He would not give up until you took time to sit down and let him get in your lap. And of course, it was better for the person than the cat.

When we lived on the Eastern Shore of Maryland, Poo was getting on in years, but he still had the curiosity of a kitten. He napped more, and didn't leap quite so high as he once had, but he was still very much a cat in charge of his territory. One unforgettable day his curiosity got him into a jam that might have cost him his life and me my sanity. It happened like this: In the middle of winter, we had not a snowstorm but a howling blizzard. The wind blew from the river, stirring the incessant snow into a thick, engulfing white cloud. The wind rattled the windows and beat against the walls. Two rocking chairs on the screened porch rocked madly in the wind, as though occupied by fiends, until we went outside and propped them against the wall. The temperature kept dropping and we huddled by the fire, waiting out the storm. It did not let up. Finally, we went to bed. Next morning I woke up to the sound of dripping water.

As I gradually awakened, I felt as though I were paralyzed, as though I couldn't move my arms and legs. It was then that I realized that all four of the Labs had left their rugs on the floor and joined us on the king-size bed. They were snuggled close to our bodies. The covers were pulled tightly over Kenneth and me. He must have heard the water, too, because he tried to get up. "What the hell is going on?" he grumbled, sleepily rubbing his eyes. "What are the animals doing on the bed?" We moved our feet under the covers, dislodging the dogs, rousing them from their slumber. They got down and stood round the bed, wagging their tails. Poo didn't budge.

"It's freezing in here. The heat's off." Kenneth snatched his closet door open and said, "What a mess. My clothes are sopping wet, and there's water on the floor. A pipe has burst. Still dripping." He put on the clothes he'd dropped on a chair the night before. And that was how the day began.

We built a roaring fire in the living room and boiled a kettle of water over the fire. Fortunately, the telephone was working. With a mug of hot tea standing by, Kenneth rang up Earl Coleman, a waterman who lived in the cottage down the lane. Kenneth and Earl had a brief conversation.

"Earl said he'll come down with wrenches and pipe, but the snow is knee deep, deeper in other places. I'll have to go meet him and help with the load." Bundling into a hooded coat, Kenneth stepped out the back door. In a moment he was out of sight in the thick, misty, whirling snow. Before too long, huffing and puffing, with snow all over them, Kenneth and Earl stamped into the kitchen. They warmed themselves by the fire for a while before trudging to the cold upstairs, where the pipe had broken. The dogs and I stayed by the fire. I did not realize it, but Poo followed the men.

The old farmhouse had hot-water heat. When Earl and Kenneth removed a heat register from the wall in order to expose the pipes near the root of the problem, they discovered what had happened. The strong wind had loosened a piece of siding just enough to let the freezing air get to a section of pipe. It had frozen in that spot, and burst. It burst just above Kenneth's closet, and the escaping water had drained through the ceiling and to the floor below. If the men could remove the broken section of pipe, and cap the two exposed ends in the wall, we could have heat in the part of the house nearest the furnace. Half a loaf sounded wonderful in a blizzard! While they were wrestling with the pipe, or fetching tools, they did not notice Poo slip silently into the opening and scurry into the narrow space between the outside and inside walls. There was no insulation between the walls, so off the cat went on his narrow path, in search of who knows what. Adventure? Mice? Freedom? Kenneth and Earl successfully finished the temporary plumbing job and replaced the grid in the wall, sealing the cat inside. They came downstairs, happy with a job well done, in search of warmth and a cup of hot tea. While I put the kettle on, they got the furnace going again. The sound of the noisy furnace was like a chorus from heaven.

We were seated by the fire, talking about the storm, and speculating on how long it would keep up, when we heard a frightened, forlorn "MeeeeOw!"

"That's Poo," I said. "Sounds like he's outside."

"He's not outside in this blizzard," Kenneth said, getting up and walking toward the sound. Like a sudden squall on the bay, the shock hit us all at the same time: "He's in the wall!" The seriousness of the situation was clear. The cat had walked from one side of the house to the other, jumping up and squeezing between a chimney and the inside wall in the process. He had made his way to the opposite side of the house, where there was no wall register. The space between the inside and outside walls was so narrow, I didn't see how the big cat could turn around. I pounded on the wall, and Poo wailed in return. We hurried upstairs and removed the register where Earl and Kenneth had been at work. I stuck my head in the opening and called and whistled until I was breathless. Kenneth called and whistled. In the distance, we could hear Poo answering us from the spot where he seemed to be stuck.

"He can't turn around," I said, near tears. "And he may be too tired and scared to squeeze past that chimney again."

I knew Kenneth was worried about the cat too, but suddenly he started to laugh. I was furious and distraught. "How can you laugh at a time like this?" I stormed. Kenneth wiped his eyes, gulping back laughter. "That damn cat," Kenneth said, "this beats all his tricks. He's catty-cornered!" And he began to laugh again. I noticed Earl was stifling laughter, too. I got down on my hands and knees, stuck my head inside the wall and yelled, "Poo, if you don't turn around and come back here, you're going to freeze in those walls." Kenneth and Earl had retreated downstairs, but I persisted in calling the cat. My face was cold from the wind coming under the siding. I heard

Kenneth tromping back upstairs. He patted me on my derriere and said, "Don't worry, Jo. We can get him out of the wall this spring." I jumped up with fire in my eyes and saw Kenneth standing there with an open can of sardines.

"Let's try this," he said, placing the can of smelly fish just inside the opening in the wall. "Now you come down and get warm, and don't worry. If we have to, Earl and I will break through the wall and get the blasted cat out."

My anger subsided, and I said, "I just can't stand it if something happens to Poo."

"Neither can I," Kenneth said, taking my hand. "I've gotten used to the damned old curmudgeon."

We went downstairs, and Kenneth poured us all a toddy. I fidgeted, worrying about Poo. He had grown silent. Not a meow was to be heard.

"Do you think he's frozen?" I asked in alarm. "Maybe he's died in there. Maybe you'd better start making a hole in the wall right now."

"Give a little time," Kenneth said. I slumped on the couch. I sat with my back to the stairs.

"Well, hello there," Kenneth said. I whirled around just as Poo leaped on the couch. He was covered with spiderwebs and soot. He licked his whiskers. He smelled strongly of sardines.

Tar

Tar was our first Labrador retriever. He was sturdily built, with a noble head, a thick and glossy black coat, and a stout otter tail. He was a companion and a field dog. Visitors who came to our door were met by Tar, most often with a boot, sock, handbag, or kitchen towel in his mouth—anything that he could retrieve quickly after the doorbell rang or someone shouted hello. His woofing did not sound too threatening when muffled by an object in his mouth, but Tar could be intimidating. We could open the back door and quietly say to Tar, "Go get 'em!" and he would charge outside, barking fiercely. I was reassured by that fact when Kenneth was away, and Tar, the cat, and I were the only inhabitants in the old stone farmhouse in Warwick, New York. Tar was protective of his "family" and his territory, but he also was friendly. He was intelligent and adaptable, and grew up as both a city and country dog.

We trained him to heel on the streets of New York. In the evening when Kenneth was about to leave his office, he'd telephone me so that Tar and I could meet him on Park Avenue. Since I knew how long it took Kenneth to walk home, I could estimate when to leave so that Tar and I would meet him partway. Tar was not troubled by pedestrians or traffic. He stayed close on a short lead. But as soon as he spotted Kenneth coming toward us, he'd start to whine. When Kenneth was a short distance away, I'd release Tar so he could bound ahead. On the way back, he'd stick close to Kenneth's knee. Sometimes when Kenneth called me from his office before coming home, I'd be in the middle of something and couldn't meet him. So when he got to our building, he'd buzz our apartment on the intercom and say, "Send 'im down." I'd attach a short lead to Tar's collar, and he'd take the handle in his mouth. There were only two apartments on our floor, and the elevator opened into the foyer. I'd lead Tar to the elevator, punch the lobby button, and send the Lab downstairs so Kenneth could take him for a walk. People in our building all knew Tar, so they weren't surprised to see him in the elevator. He would not get off until he reached the lobby and saw Kenneth waiting for him.

When my mother spent the winter with us in New York, Tar would greet her every morning in a special way. When Ma came down the hall from her bedroom, Tar would rush to her, take hold of the side of her robe, and lead her into the kitchen for her morning coffee. He never harmed her robe, just held it lightly in his mouth. As soon as they reached the kitchen, he'd turn it loose. Ma loved Tar as much as we did. When she'd arrive for her stay with us, Tar would spend the first few nights on the floor beside her bed, as a welcoming gesture. After a few days, he'd sleep in his regular place, on his dog bed in our bedroom. My mother was used to Tar because she "dog sat" for us a number of times at her farmhouse in North Carolina. When we came back to pick up Tar, he was always a little plumper, and calm. He'd greet us happily, but not wildly, the way he sometimes did when we had to board him at a kennel.

Tar was a good traveler. In fact, he was always ready to go for a ride. A couple of times we took him with us to go salmon fishing. In each case, we were staying in a cabin at a fishing camp. It was always a pleasure to have him along. On one of these trips, we put a watermelon on the back seat of the station wagon where it wouldn't roll around and break. Tar took a look at it, and sat on it, like a person sitting on a stool. When I happened to turn around and see the big black Lab sitting on the watermelon, gazing out the windows like any tourist, I began to laugh. "What's so funny?" Kenneth wanted to know. I pointed to the dog on the watermelon. Kenneth quickly turned and saw Tar. "Well, I'll be damned," he said and laughed. I took a picture of Tar perched on the melon so I could prove it was true. If Tar was along when we were transporting a melon, it became his car seat. It was Tar's habit, also, to take the place behind the steering wheel the moment a vehicle was parked and the driver got out. It was funny to see the dog sitting at the wheel, as though waiting for someone to get in the passenger's seat, so the Lab could crank up and drive off.

Anyone who believes that a house dog can't be a keen hunting dog has never lived with a Lab. Kenneth and I taught Tar to retrieve with canvas boat bumpers. He'd streak across the yard after the bumpers and bring them back, panting and eager for the game to continue. When we threw a bumper in a pond, creek, or river, he'd plunge in after it. He was a strong swimmer. Kenneth introduced Tar to pheasant hunting at the Black Meadow Club, only a few miles from our country place in New York State. His instinct to find the birds surfaced easily, and he would crisscross the woods ahead of the gunners. If he got out of range, Kenneth would command, "Hunt close," and Tar would move back. The pheasants would hide in hedgerows and coverts, often running ahead of the hunter. It is exciting sport to see a Lab overtake and flush pheasants from cover. The cock pheasant is most spectacular when he seems to spring straight up, with his startling cry—*Cok! Cok! Cok!* In a flash of brilliant color, he levels off with amazing speed. Many a gunner, surprised by the sudden flight of a pheasant, gets only a tailfeather as the bird flies toward cover. Tar always watched alertly for downed birds. He would trace the flight of one that was just winged and plunge into heavy cover to bring it to Kenneth. And he would trail a wounded bird until he could catch it, or until the gunner could finish the bird with a second shot. A wounded pheasant, with long, sharp spurs, is no easy bird to retrieve.

Tar loved pheasant hunting. He would lie in the back of the station wagon among gun cases, game vests, and boots until the wagon

turned into the bumpy lane leading to the club. Then he immediately scrambled to his feet, whining eagerly.

I think Tar knew when it was Saturday and time to go hunting, because he'd stick to Kenneth like glue. He was right with him wherever he went. When Kenneth stood a gun case beside the door while getting into his hunting jacket, Tar would station himself next to the gun and the door, so Kenneth couldn't go without him. Many years later, when Tar was having physical problems and couldn't hunt as often, he would try to get out the door with Kenneth anyway. It was heartbreaking to hear him cry, and to see him race from window to window for a glimpse of the departing wagon.

Tar took to duck and goose hunting, too. He was always ready to go, no matter how cold and miserable the weather. He'd leap into a truck with a load of decoys, or hunker close to you on an amphibious "weasel" that transported hunters, retrievers, and equipment to a water blind. In a pit blind dug into a cornfield, he'd be quiet, look up at the cover over the pit, and listen for a flock of oncoming geese. When the geese came near, he'd shiver with excitement. Once the lid was thrown back, he'd scramble out of a pit blind and race across corn stubble to a fallen goose. But Tar did not like retrieving geese. If he had any fault, that was it. He'd go straight to the fallen bird, as though pointing it out. He'd pick it up, run back toward the blind for a distance, and then drop the goose, coughing down and feathers out of his mouth as he trotted back to the blind. He just didn't like the taste of goose down, and those were big, heavy birds. So we accepted it and retrieved our own birds from the fields. If we were gunning from a water blind, he'd snappily retrieve ducks, but some other retriever had to go for geese!

Tar was wonderful company. He loved going for walks to the river and splashing in the reedy shallows. He loved going to the beach and jumping in the waves and playing Frisbee. He was patient and reliable with children. He would curl up on the sofa or bed with you, if allowed. Sometimes he napped in those comfortable places without invitation. If you should cry, he would put his head in your lap, watching you and slowly wagging his tail. He was always close by. He was a retriever you always had to stop, because he'd run too long and swim too far. When our pets live in our home, we get to know their ways, their personalities. Tar was a member of our family. He was loving and loyal. When my vision dimmed, Tar seemed to understand, and would move out of my way, whereas before I had always stepped over him when he was sprawled on the floor. If I happened to glimpse him on the floor, I'd say, "I see you, Tar," and he'd stay put and I'd step over him.

Kenneth and Tar had that special relationship of hunting companions. Of all things, Tar liked hunting best. He had all the best qualities of his breed, the Labrador retriever. He was fine, as fine a dog as ever lived.

The Rest of the Pack

We called her Nikki. Later we called her Nikki the Slippery Noodle when it had been proven time and again that she could slip out of anywhere. There was no way to contain her. Nikki was not your classic Labrador retriever. She was slim, and her muzzle and tail were too long for her to be called a perfect Lab, but she was beautiful in her own way. She was trim and tidy, athletic and competitive. She loved the water more than any of our other dogs, and on a summer day, she would sail over the kennel fence and take a few laps in the pool. If Kenneth or I should happen to leave the house in a swimsuit, Nikki was sure to see us. She'd fuss and fuss, hoping we'd let her join us. We usually did, because if we didn't, she'd jump the fence anyway.

Nikki was gentle of nature and very affectionate. It would not do to scold her except in the mildest way because she would cringe and look perfectly miserable. And there were plenty of times when we wished to scold Nikki. Like the times, on the Eastern Shore of Maryland, when she'd escape her kennel and go explore the middle of the frozen Choptank River. In winter I lived in constant fear that she would get out on the ice and slip through. We covered her kennel, but she'd climb the fence and force her face through the wire until she could get out. We tried to keep an eye on her because we were so afraid she would injure herself, but we couldn't watch her every minute.

Once, when she was just six months old, she was riding in the Jeep with Kenneth. The window on his side was open. He drove into the yard at the Black Meadow Club, and Nikki spotted some other dogs there. Before Kenneth realized what had happened, Nikki leaped past him and out the window. She was quick enough to do that. Unfortunately, she jammed her right front leg, just for an instant, in the outside door handle. It caught there long enough to crack the bone. The poor thing spent the next few months wearing a cast. To tell the truth, the cast didn't seem to slow her down very much. We kept her in the house, and she'd thump around, tail wagging, like nothing was wrong.

Nikki jumped higher and ran more quickly than the other Labs. She was not gun shy, but she was terrified of thunder and lightning. The moment a storm came up, we'd bring her inside, and try to keep her calm. The vet suggested we give her a tranquilizer when we knew a storm was coming, but sometimes storms would happen so quickly there wouldn't be time. With each storm, Nikki went wild. She'd race around the house, and if we didn't hold on to her, she'd leap out a window. Right through a screen. It was a full-time job trying to keep her safe.

While we lived at our farm in New York State, Nikki would slip off at every opportunity to explore the fields behind the barn. If I went to the kennel and she wasn't there, or if one minute she was at my side and the next minute nowhere to be seen—I knew where to look. She'd be poking around in the field, sniffing out field mice, and giving vent to her wanderlust. She was a difficult dog in her determination to be out and running all the time, but she was a very sweet-natured pet. She liked nothing better than curling up close to you, and would sit beside your chair for as long as you would pet her. (Unless, of course, there was a storm.)

Shortly before we moved to Maryland, Nikki came in season, so we locked her in a single kennel run. We felt that it would be safe and secure—and that she wouldn't be able to get out. We were wrong. One day while Kenneth and I ran an errand, the yard man came to mow the lawn. When we got home, the man shut off the mower and walked over to meet us. We exchanged greetings. He wiped his brow with a bright-red bandanna and said, "That little black dog came around the barn just after I drove up. I knew she wasn't supposed to be loose. I called her and she came over to me, friendly as anything." He finished mopping his forehead, stuffed the bandanna in his hip pocket.

"Where'd she go?" Kenneth asked, his own brow creasing with worry.

"Oh, she's fine. I led her right over there and put her right back in the kennel. Haven't seen her since. Guess she's still there."

"Uh-oh!" I said, noticing the direction the gardener pointed. Kenneth was ahead of me. He hurried over to the row of gates. The yard man had unwittingly closed Nikki in a run with Jedediah. When Kenneth opened the gate, she came running out, with Jedediah in pursuit. We feared it was too late. As it turned out, it was.

There came a time when friends of ours, the Snows, who owned a big, beautiful female Lab, asked to mate her with Tar. We agreed. For Tar's stud fee, we would get the pick of the litter. Somehow, there never seemed to be a question of whether we needed three Labs. We had two, so now we'd have three. The other owners called us when the pups were born. It was a big litter of ten. "Both yellows and blacks," they told us. This delighted Kenneth, because he wanted a yellow Lab. I really didn't care which color we chose, or for that matter, which sex. We kept in touch with the breeders concerning the progress of the puppies. Finally, it was time to drive to the next state and take our pick of the litter. Friends of ours from Texas were visiting at the time, so they rode with us.

When we drove into the yard of the handsome country estate, the owners had the mother of the pups and the entire litter out on the front lawn. What a sight! A light breeze was stirring, and the mother of the litter sat calmly on the perfectly tended lawn, lifting her head and ignoring the yellow and black puppies that waddled all around her on the green grass. When the four of us got out of the station wagon, the Snows came down the lawn to greet us. We hurried over to the puppies. The big female stood, facing us, ready to protect her litter from strangers. She did not growl, but she was watchful. Her owners calmed her so we could approach. Kenneth stooped down and immediately picked up the biggest yellow puppy.

"She's pretty, isn't she?" Joan Snow commented. "She's big for a female."

"She's perfect!" Kenneth said, holding the fat puppy like a child holds his favorite teddy bear. I had spotted a lively, pudgy black male pup, and the moment I saw him, I thought, "There's Jedediah," as though I knew his name. Still holding the plump yellow pup, Kenneth looked at me and said, "We'll take him, too." Our friends from Texas were amused, but said nothing. And that is how Drambuie and Jedediah, soon shortened to "Buie" and "Jed," came to join our family.

It was very odd how Jedediah's name popped into my mind the moment I saw him. I never had known anyone with that name, and certainly hadn't planned to pick up two puppies. But when I saw him, I knew his name. Jed was a big-footed, clumsy puppy. He was always underfoot and was very easy to housebreak. He grew to be a very big Lab. He was bigger than Tar, and reminded us of the character Ferdinand the Bull, because he looked so dangerous, yet was so sweet. It is absolutely true that if I put a bouquet of flowers on a low table, Jedediah would sniff them. His hunting instincts were good, but if there ever was such a thing as a "laid-back" dog, Jed was it. He loved napping in the sun. If fact, he loved napping anywhere. Sometimes in winter, Kenneth would stretch out on the rug in front of the fireplace, to rest his tired back after a day afield. It would not be long before Jed was stretched out close beside him, and would warn off any of the other Labs who had similar notions with a low, quiet, but very serious growl.

Jed loved apples. If anyone should be eating one, Jed would hang around and wag his tail and worry you until you gave him an apple. He'd trot off with it and chomp on it. Also, in the fall, when apples dropped on the ground from the

trees in the backyard, Jed would pick one up and take it off and eat it. I discovered he liked to play with an English pea. Not the whole pod. Just one pea. In Maryland, in summer, we'd often pick fresh peas. I'd sit down in a chair to shell them with a bowl in my lap and Jed would come place his head there too, if there was room, or he'd nudge me.

On a whim, I once handed him a single, fat, round green pea. He took it in his mouth, walked away, and threw the pea in the air. When it landed, he chased it, picked it up by placing his muzzle flat against the floor, and continued his game until he either smashed the pea or accidentally bit it. Then he came back for another, the first of many. It was funny to see that big, tough-looking Lab playing with a pea. I'd have to go round the house afterwards and collect the smashed green peas. If I happened to be sitting in a chair snapping green beans, he paid no attention. He knew when I was shelling peas. And he'd pester anyone who was shelling peas until he was handed one of the green legumes.

I'll never forget a late afternoon in the fall when Kenneth and I took Jed for a romp in the meadow at the gun club. The four-month-old pup was running around in the tall, thick grass when a pair of pheasants jumped up. Kenneth shot a perfect double, and Jed struck out for the first downed bird. We were amazed to see him return with the cock pheasant. Then he went snuffling around until he found the second bird, but he waited, wagging his tail, until we came over and picked the pheasant up. But it was a pretty flashy start for a four-month-old pup. Jed was a reliable, enthusiastic hunting dog and retriever, but he never had the zest for it that Tar did. The only problem with Jed as a retriever was that he would swim after a wounded bird even when he was commanded to return. He was headstrong about that, and it was very dangerous when the water was freezing cold. He could easily have given out and slipped below the surface. More than once, Kenneth had to get into a motor boat and go get Jed before he had a chance to exhaust himself.

Buie was such a pretty puppy that everyone wanted to pick her up. She became a truly beautiful female, with a wonderful head, fine conformation, and a thick golden coat. She had those meltingly friendly eyes of a Lab, and charmed everybody. Buie was very competitive among the rest of the pack, but she had no interest in hunting. She did not like guns or dead birds, and was very reluctant to spend time in duck blinds. The first time Kenneth and I took her goose hunting, we were in a pit blind. At the first volley of gunshot, Buie dove under me and hid as much of her big body as she could in the wooden crate on which I had been sitting. She wanted nothing to do with the whole scene. All she wanted to do was be a friendly, loving house dog. She was a fine companion on a walk. She loved hunting field mice, swimming anywhere there was water, and chasing squirrels up a tree. She would happily join you in a dinghy for a row along the shoreline, and was the first to load when the tailgate of the station wagon was lowered. She was a great watchdog, and I feel sure she would have defended us well. Buie was independent and her very own "girl."

I have met a few people I didn't care for, and dogs that were not friendly, but I have never met a Labrador retriever I didn't like. Each of our Labs had distinct personalities, but they all were friendly, gentle with children, and wonderful pets. Considering their intelligence and equally good nature, it is understandable that so many Labrador retrievers serve as Seeing Eye dogs.

Nicodemus Hyde

It was at the house on Otter Pond that I was adopted by Nicodemus Hyde. Nicodemus was a burly, fearless Labrador retriever who was blind in one eye. Kenneth and I spent one year in the Victorian cottage overlooking Otter Pond on Gibson Island, Maryland, following my surgery at Johns Hopkins hospital in Baltimore, in which a tumor was removed from my optic nerve. The procedure left me totally blind in my left eye, and with very little vision in my right. When Nicodemus and I met, I swear to all (with tongue in cheek) that Nicodemus recognized that we were kindred spirits with similar problems, and he felt responsible for my rehabilitation.

Bryden Hyde, a prominent architect, and his wife, Dianna, were our landlords. Bryden's elderly mother had lived in the cottage, but had recently moved. Nicodemus was accustomed to having the run of the place, and when we moved in with our own dogs and cat, Nicodemus came to visit. He'd stop at the big, portable kennel where Nikki, Jedediah, and Buie stayed, just a short distance from the house. They barked so loudly that the rhododendrons that concealed the kennel fairly shuddered from the uproar. I fear this did not endear us to nearby residents on the bucolic island. Also, cats were not popular with local bird-watchers, and in spite of the fact that our Poo was an "inside" cat, I had prepared for any disapproving callers the alibi that "Poo is a rare, orange Tasmanian squirrel that looks a lot like a common housecat." But I digress. Nicodemus went about his rehabilitative duties doggedly. When finished greeting the dogs outside, he'd trot over to the front door, come up the steps, and stand at the louvered door, patiently waiting to be let in. As soon as Tar got a whiff of Nicodemus outside the front door, he'd race down the hall to confront the intruder. Nose to nose with the door as a barrier, they'd compete in a ferocious growling match. The growling usually was brief and ceremonial. They'd soon tire of it and Tar would retire to the sunporch at the back of the house, and Nicodemus would sprawl on the front porch.

When I began, very tentatively, to walk about the island, using a short cane to find my way, Nicodemus was right with me. I'd walk to the tennis courts with the stocky Lab close on my heels. We'd pause and listen to the hollow sound of the tennis balls being struck. I imagine we looked as forlorn as two kids not chosen for the team at a pickup ball game. Nicodemus, I discovered, was fond of brawling. He'd tear out after any dog unfortunate enough to be in his path. These bouts were mostly noise and territorial scuffling, but they sounded fearsome. I imagine the residents of the island could trace our path by the sound of the dog fights.

I liked Nicodemus and enjoyed his company, but the encounters along the way were nerve-racking. So, before setting out on a walk, I'd peek out to see if Nicodemus was around. If I didn't see him, I'd tiptoe across the yard to the road. But Nicodemus always found out. I'd hear him trotting up behind me. Other times, he'd take a shortcut and overtake me. Sometimes I'd hear him panting, as he rested beside the road, waiting for me to catch up. If I stumbled, Nicodemus would stop and wait until I regained my footing.

On these walks, I often met a lady of delicate build and manner, with soft grey hair framing her pleasant face. She was a Christian Scientist, she explained. After an exchange of pleasantries, she'd bring up the matter of healing by faith. She troubled herself to bring to the cottage a number of Mary Baker Eddy recordings for my edification. I was unaware that this kind lady had a dog, until the unfortunate day Nicodemus and I met her and her miniature poodle, Biscuit, on the road. I couldn't see the tiny dog, so when I heard Nicodemus growl his battle cry, for an astonished moment I thought the devil-may-care old Lab was growling at me or the other lady. Then, with utter dismay, I heard Biscuit's terrified scream as Nicodemus chased him into the bushes. I ran toward the racket and smacked Nicodemus's stout rump with my cane. It startled him. He whirled around, looking at me in surprise. This gave Biscuit time enough to streak toward home, with his mistress racing after him at a sprightly pace. I caught Nicodemus by the collar, and he calmed down immediately, once more my friendly hell-raising companion. Biscuit was not really hurt, but was badly scared. Subsequently, some rancorous exchanges took place between dog owners. But when I went walking again, Nicodemus trotted beside me as if he were on duty.

If there was anything Nicodemus liked better than exploring the island and terrifying other dogs, it was swimming in Otter Pond. Our cottage overlooked the pond and had a floating dock behind it. I

didn't usually go swimming alone, but one hot day I couldn't resist. I
put on my swimsuit, grabbed a towel, and slipped out the side door.
Creeping cautiously down the sloping bank, ducking under overhang-
ing rhododendrons, I stepped onto the sunny, warm dock and sat
down at the edge, my legs dangling in the water. It was quiet, peace-
ful, wonderful. Holding the ladder, I eased into the water. Just as I
took a few lazy strokes away from the dock, I heard something crashing through the bushes. Nicodemus shot out of the underbrush, clattered across the dock, looked around, spotted me, and did a Labrador
bellyflop into the pond. He nearly landed on me and began paddling
around. It was clear that the big dog's delight at being in the water
might very well swamp me. So I headed back to the dock with
Nicodemus in my wake. I climbed out and sat on the warm boards
while the retriever swam a few more noisy laps before he scrambled
ashore. He hurried back to the dock, and standing beside me, shook
mightily.

It was impossible not to love Nicodemus—he was such a lov-
able character. During that difficult year, Nicodemus was constantly
around, though he always went home at night. Sometimes he'd come
for an early morning visit, other times he'd come late, but he almost
always checked in some time during the day. And if I did go swimming or for a walk, he was there, like magic. Nicodemus had lessons
to teach, if one took notice. He was independent, but loyal. Good
qualities in dogs or people. He was companionable. And he lived in
the moment, and was always ready for adventure. Nicodemus was a
dog of many virtues, and in my opinion, any faults were of no conse-
quence. Nicodemus was never, never boring.

Crows and Scarecrows

Every now and then, when I was a child, my parents would say, "Let's ride over to Sandy Grove." "Sandy Grove" was Sandy Grove Presbyterian Church, built by Scottish settlers who came up the Cape Fear River in North Carolina and then moved inland forty miles or so to the rolling terrain of the pinelands. Those piney forests were taken over years ago by the United States government, and became part of Ft. Bragg Military Reservation. The old white clapboard church was left in isolation when the people were displaced by the reservation, but it was well cared for over the years. To a child, it was a lonesome-looking place, yet I loved tagging along with my folks on the ride through the woods on (then) sandy roads. We'd visit the early settlers, and, in fact, my mother had a sister laid to rest in the cemetery behind the church.

It was those trips to Sandy Grove that stirred in me an enduring affection for crows. When we drove into the white-sand churchyard and got out of the car, there always was, to me, a deep stillness, tinged with melancholy even on the sunniest day. We could hear every insect clearly, every distant birdsong, and the soft whispering of wind in the tall pines. Our voices sounded very small in that vast silence. After strolling around the venerable church, we'd always walk out to the cemetery, and my parents would notice this gravestone or that, reading the names of early settlers who were laid to rest at Sandy Grove. I tiptoed among the gravestones, fearing that I might commit the discourtesy of accidentally stepping on someone's grave. And unfailingly, there would be the loud and raucous cawing of crows high above us. Those crows were a friendly sound in that quiet place.

Ever since that time, I have been fond of crows, and every time I hear "Caw! Caw!" I am cheered. The truth is that even before those trips to Sandy Grove, I was fascinated by the sight and sound of crows around our farm and in the pine woods. I still love the sight of the big birds, glossy black and calling to one another, flying in small flocks across the sky. They seem to fly so casually, up there where there are no rules of the road. They tumble, tilt, and sail, their ebony feathers shining iridescent in the sun.

Crows are charming to me because they appear in the oddest places. I got out of the car in a sprawling parking lot at a shopping mall one day, and was delighted to hear crows overhead. They seemed

to be everywhere! Crows like to build their nests (March through May) in trees at least sixty feet tall, preferably pines or cedars. They build deep, bulky nests high up in the branches—nests so well concealed they are difficult, if not impossible, to see from the ground. The eggs are speckled white, and broods are generally from three to seven chicks. Both parents care for the chicks, who stay with their parents throughout the summer.

Crows are kin to the jays, ravens, and nutcrackers, and are very intelligent birds. I have been told that young crows make excellent pets, though I am not suggesting this, unless for some irreversible reason a chick needs to be taken in. A young chick does not eat much at a time, but he must have food equal to one-half his body weight per day in order to survive. (Some people who rescue young crows are not aware of this, and can inadvertently let a chick starve to death.) It is not long, however, before a crow can consume food equal to its full body weight.

It is said that young crows are easy to train, and even to teach tricks and simple games. There are documented cases of crows rolling balls with children, and striding up and down a seesaw that is in use, actually riding one end and then the other. When tamed crows grow older, they can become even more mischievous. I read about a pet crow that would steal his mistress's thimbles, and had the naughty habit of pinching clothespins off the clothesline and burying them. How irritating if you had wash on the line! But there is something about the rapscallion crow that is dear to me.

Farmers beleaguered by hungry crows are not apt to find them so endearing. They are resourceful when it comes to eating, as more than 156 items have been listed as palatable to the crow. Farmers know only too well that they relish corn, and are inordinately fond of pecking holes in watermelons and cantaloupes for the delicacy within. Crows are so clever and dexterous that they can go into a patch of field peas, strip the shells off the vines, open them, and eat the peas out of the shells. And they like pecans almost as much as squirrels do. It is said that crows are marauders of other birds' nests in order to eat the eggs. But, according to one study, of the 108 crows that were examined, only one had evidence of eggs in its stomach. Crows will kill and eat reptiles, frogs, and toads. It is true that crows will feast freely on farmers' crops and the backyard garden as well, but they also consume a tremendous number of insects. They eat May beetles and their grubs, wire worms, caterpillars, and cutworms, to name a few. So it's only fair to give the rascals their due for their good habits.

Ravens and crows share many of the same characteristics. They have a throaty, harsh call that is more like "Car! Car!" than a cawing sound. Fish crows are residents of the Eastern shores, and their diet consists of fish, crabs, and even carrion that washes ashore. Not having studied crows carefully, I was surprised the first time I saw what looked like a small common crow strutting on a beach—the territory of plovers, sandpipers, terns, and gulls. I quickly learned that it was a fish crow who lives in the marshlands.

Crows are sensible birds in many ways. When they are feeding, as well as at other times, they appoint a sentinel to keep an eye out for trouble. The sentinel sounds the alarm if anything or anyone approaches. An older, more experienced bird is usually the sentinel, but woe betide the one that drifts off to sleep or lets his guard down in any way, for the flock will punish him. In winter, flocks of crows will roost together, often in rookeries of quite a large size.

Whenever I hear a crow, I always look up, hoping to see the jaunty bird in flight. I hear crows when I step out on the back porch, when walking in the woods, at the edge of town, along a river, beside the sea, and often at lonely moments. One year when Kenneth and I were visiting St. David's on the coast of Wales, we were walking toward the wonderful cathedral there, when a great noise, incessant and throatily familiar, came from a rooftop. The roof was thick with ravens, and they were being their naturally gregarious selves. I smiled, and as we approached the cathedral, thought of Sandy Grove.

SCARECROW

Scarecrow, Scarecrow,
As magical as the unicorn
In his circled fence—
Where do you come from?
From whimsy that survives deep
In a farmer's heart,
And like a baby crow
Flies up by instinct?

Field-rough hands
Form your stalky frame,
Your outstretched arms.
With an inward, defiant smile
Your magical raiment
Is gathered.

There you stand
In sun and rain, Scarecrow,
Stolid in hay-stuffed overalls,
Denim shirt and wide straw hat.
A red bandanna in your hand
Flutters in every breeze,

Shooing the crows away
From the tall, green corn.

And here you seem
To crouch, Scarecrow.
So short you are,
In a small, faded dress
And a country bonnet.
Touchingly valiant, you are,
Guarding the tomatoes and peas
In a summer garden.

In a field of tangled vines
And fattening watermelons,
You are tall, tall, tall.
Three of you there are,
In your tattered finery
And hat, hat, hat.

You are as magical
As the unicorn,
Who has leapt the circle
And runs loose,

Grazing among the melons,
Drawn by your magic.

You are the soil-man's
Faint hope for fair play,
His whimsical jeer
At the ebony crows—
Who fly and caw,
And circle above you,
And circle above—
And as if by magic
The sentinel crow
Alights on your arm
And comfortably watchful, waits—
While the rest of the flock
Feeds.

HEARTH AND HOME

Near the camouflage gear is a wall basket,
filled to overflowing with gloves and knit hats.
On the floor beneath it is a big,
sturdy basket for boots. In this same basket there
is sure to be a ragged cotton towel for giving the
old Labrador a quick drying
after an outing in rain or sleet.
The towel is spread over the basket to dry.
Also in this ideal country pantry, the window
frame is wide enough to accommodate a hand-
powered coffee grinder.
Close at hand will be jars of coffee beans to grind
and blend. The windowsill is broad and sunny,
perfect for plant cuttings and seedling trays.
Stoneware crocks are in a row along one wall.
Many old baskets hang from the ceiling,
field glasses and bird book stand by the window,
and there are shelves and shelves filled with cookbooks. Handiest of all, on a hook by the pantry
door, hangs a faded, well-broken-in,
blue wool sweater.

Old Stone House

There is a point, when you are renovating an old stone farm-house, at which you doubt your sanity. That point came for me the day when I was prying and pounding lath and plaster from the dining-room ceiling. Wearing a bandanna over my hair, clothes covered with grime that had come down with the ceiling, and with layers of dirt on my face, I climbed the ladder and smacked the old plaster with a wrecking bar and waited as the pieces thundered to the floor. Then I advanced to pry lath loose. I was looking up to see if it was coming down, when it gave way, and a shower of old corncobs and a desic-cated mouse carcass fell down on my head. I jumped off the ladder, brushing my face, and let out a short, fervent scream of irritation, weariness, and dismay. The dining-room floor was a pile of rubble, old plaster, lath, sooty dirt, and now—corncobs and a mouse body. We had already removed two other ceilings—the first, squares of celotex; the second, large wooden rectangles that had been painted a dismal green. As I stood there tired and dirty, looking at the rubble that would have to be removed and the ceiling that was left to take down, I realized that it was only the beginning of what had to be done in that room—and that there were other rooms to be dealt with as well. "I think you've lost your mind," I said to myself. "Why would any sane person get mixed up in such an undertaking?"

To add to my sense of futility and craziness, Kenneth had taken a few days off from the back-breaking labor to go trout fishing with friends. He had urged me to take a few days off, too, but part of the "old stone house madness" was the compulsion I felt to finish the renovation and spend the rest of our days like regular people who weren't always hammering, scraping, painting, papering, and spending a fortune at the hardware store. At that particular moment, I threw the wrecking bar down in the rubble and walked out. I had a bath and a long nap. After the nap, I felt better, but still wondered if Kenneth and I had both lost our minds.

We were removing the ceilings in order to expose the aged chestnut beams, removing layers of paint from an original corner cupboard, having floors sanded upstairs, and having rough carpentry done. When we weren't wrestling with inside work, we were painting the exterior, with help whenever we could get it. In addition, the old concrete pool leaked like a sinking ship, and professionals were administering pricey first aid to it. We were doing most of the work ourselves, and that was enough to make anyone doubt their sanity.

It didn't take me long to realize that the sane thing to do was to finish the job, but without working ourselves into the ground. We needed to slow the pace, which was what Kenneth had said all along, but I had a vision that I was eager to see become reality.

When we finished the work, it looked wonderful to us, and we knew why we had loved the old stone house from the very beginning. We had rented the house a couple of winters when the owner was away, and had enjoyed it. When it came on the market, we didn't hesitate. We bought it and started making plans. It was a handsome, simple house that, we believe, was built by Huguenot builders. It had a clapboard addition at one end, which was added later, but the date 1795 was carved in a chimney stone.

It is in the register of historic stone houses in Orange County, New York. It had been built close enough to the road for riders to step off their mounts on a block by the stone steps leading to the front yard, or for passengers in a buggy or coach to do the same thing. After more than a century, the narrow country road was paved and widened, and the front of the house was very near the highway. The back of the house, however, had a fine view of fields, and on the right, a swift creek. There was a barn and a potting shed, kennels, a corncrib, and a big shed. A small patio and screened porch were at the back of the house. The pool was between the patio and the long slope that pitched toward the creek.

A circular driveway at the kitchen end of the house was where everyone came in. No one ever used the huge old front door that was held in place by its original strap hinges. There was another small entry and a door into the dining room, and strangers sometimes came there and actually rang the sleigh bells hanging on the door. Everyone else came in through the small, narrow kitchen, thence to the dining room and into the living room. It was a house that suited us.

The kitchen was small, but there was an adjacent pantry that gave additional space. The dishwasher and storage cabinets were in there. We painted all the old wooden cupboards a warm, sunny gold, and put burlap on the walls. When the dining room was done, the lower walls and molding were slate blue, the walls above were white. Kenneth had extracted or cut off dozens of handmade, headless nails from the overhead beams. The nails led us to believe the beam had been used before—perhaps in another house or barn. Kenneth cleaned the beams. They looked strong and fitting in the room. We hung many baskets from them, and put plants in the bay window that faced the front of the house. The old cupboard was tawny wood, once it was cleaned, sanded, waxed, and ready to hold my collection of Bennington pottery. The mantel, which we refinished, was pumpkin pine, and looked just right against the stone fireplace. On the back of the living room fireplace was its twin, in a small room that we changed to a library. The two fireplaces shared the stone chimney that went from cellar to housetop. We furnished our home mostly with antiques. When Kenneth and I were alone, we spent most of our time in the library, where we had built floor-to-ceiling bookshelves, and a slightly wider shelf in one bookcase to accommodate the television set. On summer evenings, we opened the window and could hear the brook. On winter evenings, we built a cozy fire and settled in comfortable chairs. There was a bathroom in the front hall, and narrow stairs leading to the second floor.

Wider stairs led from the dining room to the bedrooms. There were two small bedrooms on the right of the stairs, and a big, central bedroom with a sloping ceiling and dormer windows at the front of the house. A simple plank door led from the center bedroom into a huge attic, where the pegged beams could be seen. All over the house there were wide-board floors, some of which we had refinished. The board floor of the attic was aged and stained. The chimney was exposed in the attic, with a few small open chinks that let out tiny puffs of smoke when a fire was burning in a fireplace downstairs. Someone told me that homesteaders often hung their cured meats in the attic, and the smoke would enhance its flavor. I don't know if that was true, but we had the chimney inspected, and the inspectors said that it was safe, and the small amount of smoke in the big, unheated attic was harmless. Maybe it was a form of mothproofing!

The center bedroom was ours, and to the right was another small bedroom with space for a rope bed. I removed all the old wallpaper in that room, painted the walls white, and stenciled them. With a woven blue coverlet on the bed, and an antique chest and chair, it was a pretty, though less than spacious, guest room. A door led from the bedroom into a paneled gun room and the stairs leading to the downstairs bathroom. Negotiating the narrow stairs was not easy if one happened to be in a hurry. The four bedrooms shared a bath at the end of the hall, which was tucked under a dormer. All the fixtures were very close together. A bather in "jaybird suit" could stand with impunity in the tub, and gaze out the dormer window; and if so inclined, could converse with someone on the back lawn. To install another bath, we would have had to eliminate a room, destroy an original stone wall, or use part of the attic space. We chose to do none of these things. Houseguests had to go down the hall and sometimes downstairs to a bathroom, and they had to be careful not to bump their heads or shins. In an old stone house, it was part of the charm.

There is something special about any old house, but an old stone house has a unique aura. It speaks of endurance and craftsmanship and safety. And the old stone walls will be there to protect others, long after we depart. It seemed only a heartbeat from the day we completed the renovation there until we had to move off to Maryland. In spite of all the frustration and hard work, Kenneth and I always agreed that it was the house we loved best.

Country Comforts

When the February sky is gun-barrel gray and the sun has lost its battle with the cold, two things are sure to bring comfort: an old wool sweater and a country pantry. My aged (it's at least fifteen years old) blue cable-knit sweater is faded, with a permanent coat hook mark at the neckline from years of hanging "handy by." It droops and sags unfashionably from my shoulders, like the hug of a good friend. In a drafty old country house on an icy February day, it fortifies the spirit. Thus comforted, I set about straightening our little pantry. As I rearrange the jars of pickles and chowchow and tomatoes and jam, I note there's plenty to last until spring. One shelf is a jumble of vases and frogs for flower arranging; another is a puzzle of paint cans and thermos jugs. It is too small, and it sets me yearning for a big country pantry. Like every woman who loves home, hearth, and cooking, I fantasize about designing the perfect kitchen for my way of doing things—and every design includes a big pantry, with a window.

There was such a pantry in the farmhouse where I grew up, and it was grand. It was a sensible long pantry, wide enough to enter with arms full, and to turn around without knocking something over. Shelves started about waist level and went to the ceiling. That left room on the floor for tall tins of flour, sugar, and corn meal. There was also space for a crate of oranges, bag of potatoes, and a standing churn. Shelves were spaced in such a way that small and large objects could be stored. Jars of fruits and vegetables stood in neat rows, and a turkey-size roasting pan and a galvanized tub were stowed on a deeper shelf. In that pantry there seemed to be room for everything—jars, bags, boxes, food grinders, spices, cake tins, a sewing basket, mops and brooms; dried beans and a string of peppers.

And how wonderful a country pantry smells—it is a rich blend of cinnamon and molasses and pine oil. With a window at one end it is easy to air out. A country pantry is always a favorite hiding place for Hide-and-Go-Seekers. While you're waiting to be "found," an oatmeal cookie from the cookie jar is a side benefit. In our farmhouse pantry country hams sometimes were suspended from the ceiling, lending the air a tantalizing smoky fragrance. That pantry was also a good place to hide birthday and Christmas presents, and sometimes, when unexpected company dropped in, it was a handy, temporary repository for schoolbooks or kitchen clutter.

If you have a big pantry, what delightful country pleasure it must be to step inside and easily remove a large stock pot from a capacious shelf, with no irritating struggle, no digging into the back of a gloomy cabinet. How pleasant, too, to take down from this special place herbs to go in the stock pot with other ingredients for soup. Meal planning is simplified with a pantry for storing supplies. If the power fails and roads are blocked in a winter storm, a well-stocked pantry is a godsend.

A pantry reveals a lot about the character of its keeper. Are the shelves filled with a balance of convenience foods and homemade goodies? Pruning shears hanging on a hook and a gardening encyclopedia tell you something. So does a pasta machine, or an electrical smoker and a bag of hickory chips. A high chair or stroller in a corner tells a story, as does a bag of kitty litter. A big dough bowl and several varieties of flour are surely evidence of an enthusiastic baker. While I do not suggest accuracy in character-analysis-by-pantry, it can have its revealing moments. (Better be careful who peeps into your pantry.)

So while the pot of soup chuckles on the stove, I fend off the winter chill with warm imaginings of filling my imaginary country pantry: Tall hurricane shades are safely on a top shelf, a heavy marmite on the floor, a wok and large oval copper pan hang on the wall. Earl Grey and orange pekoe tea stand shoulder to shoulder; basil and tarragon perfume the air. A basket of pinecones is in a corner, the food processor sits on a middle shelf, and camouflage parkas hang on pegs.

Near the camouflage gear is a wall basket, filled to overflowing with gloves and knit hats. On the floor beneath it is a big, sturdy basket for boots. In this same basket there is sure to be a ragged cotton towel for giving the old Labrador a quick drying after an outing in rain or sleet. The towel is spread over the basket to dry. Also in this ideal country pantry, the window frame is wide enough to accommodate a hand-powered coffee grinder. Close at hand will be jars of coffee beans to grind and blend. The windowsill is broad and sunny, perfect for plant cuttings and seedling trays.

Stoneware crocks are in a row along one wall. Many old baskets hang from the ceiling, field glasses and bird book stand by the window, and there are shelves and shelves filled with cookbooks. Handiest of all, on a hook by the pantry door, hangs a faded, well-broken-in, blue wool sweater.

My Favorite Cookware

Steam is condensing on the windows, so I wipe a pane clear to see my husband handing out biscuits to the Labs after their morning run. The wind has hauled around to the northeast and is unfriendly enough to snatch the hat right off your head. The dogs are not reluctant to go back into their snug houses today. It is a good day for cooking.

Getting in a stew over a stewpot is admittedly ridiculous, but I've been known to do it. My husband and I both enjoy cooking, and we both appreciate the value of good pots and pans. But we have widely divergent views on exactly what is needed to equip a kitchen properly, and this leads to some heated disputes. The pot debate springs up repeatedly in our house, and it has nothing whatsoever to do with that illegal weed.

Any country cook knows the value of a reliable pot in which a stew or sauce can simmer without sticking or burning. That same cook will carefully assemble cookware through the years. My problem, according to my nearest and dearest critic, is that I am loyal to an old pot that he considers a candidate for the trash heap. Indeed, he once had the effrontery to relegate it to the role of watering pail, until I discovered this travesty and rescued it. He has not pinched the pot again, but I see him looking at it the way one might gaze at a bug in the soup. "It's not efficient," he tells me. "It will hold a dozen ears of corn without crowding," I tell him. "It takes too long to boil," he points out. "I'm in no hurry," I counter. "It's old and dented," he goes on. "Patina," is my reply. "It's ugly," he says. " Me, too," I answer, "what the heck?" We grin. "I'm going to work." He shrugs on his camouflage jacket and opens the kitchen door, letting in a blast of cold air. "What are you going to do today?" he asks. "Wrestle with cassoulet," I tell him, "so I'll be cooking beans in you-know-what-pot." "That ought to take all day" is his parting shot. "Bye."

He's right in all his criticisms of that old pot, but I am as attached to that pot as a baby is to a favorite blanket. I don't even remember where the pot came from—perhaps my mother's pantry, or a junk shop—who knows? But in spite of its irritating habit of taking forever to boil, it is a good friend in the kitchen. It is really an open kettle, broad and medium deep. It has a few dents, but the bail handle with wooden grip is attached by handsome, old-fashioned brackets. It will, as I argued, easily hold a dozen ears of corn, or a fat hen, or a pound of vermicelli, and once it gets going, it will cluck along faithfully. So far, it is still with us: It rests right beside the best copper pots.

Another favorite is a small pot bought for a nickel at a tag sale. It has two diminutive bracket handles and a perky little lid with a wooden knob. It may have been a child's toy, but it is good-quality aluminum, and just the right size for boiling four eggs or two potatoes. Working like a child trying to do a man's job, it makes you smile. There is no dispute over this little pot.

What is disputed is just how many egg-poaching devices a country kitchen needs. "Never enough" seems to be my husband's credo. Just as he cannot pass an art gallery without stepping inside for at least a few minutes, he is inexorably drawn toward kitchen shops and housewares departments wherein egg poachers lie. We have small pots with detachable racks and cups (four-eggers, eight-eggers), and we have pots with special nonstick cups. We have circles (like jar lids) for confining perfect poached eggs, and some devices that look like metal praying mantises. These stand knee-deep in hot water; the "body" holds the egg, and the long "neck" handle is for lifting the eggs from the water. It looks for all the world as though a flock of metal bugs has landed in the poaching pan when they are used. My husband is delighted with them, naturally. He edits cookware catalogs, neatly cutting out all illustrations of egg poachers. In the pot debate, it's every man for himself.

On this cold February day, when our larder holds the ingredients needed for that savory French country dish, cassoulet, I rattle among the pots and pans, choosing the right one for braising the lamb shanks, another for browning the woodcock and spicy sausages, and still another for cooking dried beans. Cassoulet cannot be hurried, but once all the ingredients are layered and put to cook slowly in the oven, the wonderful aroma makes it all worthwhile. It is a dish to share with many hungry friends gathered around the kitchen table.

To cook the goose that will be part of the dish, I struggle to the stove with what I call the "kangaroo pot." It is a mammoth copper pot, bought by my husband over my protestation, at an antiques shop. "It's too heavy," I complained, experimentally hefting it at the shop.

"You're strong," he said, pulling the checkbook from his pocket. "It's too expensive," I suggested. "It will last forever; it's the best quality," he replied. "It's big enough for a kangaroo," I howled, losing the battle. Signing the check, he looked up and said, "Is there such a thing as a recipe for Roo Stew?"

But today, as the goose simmers among the herbs in the "kangaroo pot," I can only smile at my defeat. This pot, though unwieldy, is perfect for canning a batch of chowchow, steaming dozens of crabs, or making soup or stew for a crowd. It looks very handsome on the stove, and on casual occasions, diners are dispatched to serve themselves from the pot.

Other cookware that has enjoyed our volatile attention includes the stout and deep, cast-iron chicken fryer, which is good for dozens of cooking jobs; the well-seasoned old griddle for cooking pancakes; the flintware turkey roaster; and an enamelware pan that's just right for spice cake.

Collecting things for the kitchen is fun. Although egg poachers may appeal to some, old woodenware may appeal to others. It is difficult for me to pass by an assortment of woodenware, old or new. If I poke through a crock full of wooden implements in a favorite antiques shop, I am sure to find a spoon, a paddle, a potato masher, or a rolling pin that my kitchen "needs." Even though successful pie crust is rare in my kitchen, solid wood rolling pins are not. Old bowls and dough trays are simple country pleasures that come in many sizes if you look long enough. And there's nothing like discovering a cast-iron cornstick pan in a hardware store.

The northeast wind rattles the back door like someone coming to visit. The two old dogs start to bark a greeting, but settle back down when they see no one is there but the wind, and I am just latching the door. Once again, steam condenses on the windowpanes as the cassoulet components cook in the assortment of disputed pots and pans. When the cassoulet is done, I must go into town. February is the time of St. Valentine's Day, and choosing a "surprise" for someone you love is a simple country pleasure. I wonder if the shop in town has any new egg poachers?

Spring Cleaning

SPRING CLEANING

Spring cleaning here,
I'm sorry to say,
Was not in March,
And here it is May!
March was too cold
And April too fine
To sweep remote corners
And polish and shine.
But in this fair month
I have motivation
If I don't clean house now
I'll miss summer vacation.

I have the belated spring-cleaning blues. Armed with broom, mop, bucket, and a basketful of rags and potions guaranteed to make the place sparkle and shine, I can't decide where to begin. The dustpan is missing and the vacuum cleaner rattles ominously. Moving dust around is dreary on a fine day. (My problem is really spring fever.)

I pluck a bottle from the basket and squirt blue liquid on the dirty windowpanes in the den. When they bark at visitors, the Labs make woof marks (as I call them) on the lower panels. Can I get away with washing only these sections? After a brief conscience searching, a partial cleaning seems a reasonable, labor-saving thing to do. Next, I move on to a towering stack of old newspapers piled on a brass kindling bucket. The heap lists perilously to starboard, and if I do not remove the top layers carefully, an avalanche will take place. Alas! The pile topples. Buffeted by old *Posts*, *Suns*, and *Daily Bugles*, I mutter as I give the den "a lick and a promise." I throw out straggly plants. They are hopeless, but it takes steely resolve to discard them, so strong is our urge to nurture.

Unflinchingly I move on to the utility room and start the vacuum cleaner. I listen with satisfaction as pellets of dry dog food bump up the metal tube. Deciding that this room is bound by its very nature to have utilitarian messiness, I turn to the kitchen and tackle the corner cabinet—one of those revolving cupboards that makes it possible to pack bottles, can, shakers, teapots, and other oddments in inaccessible places. Even though I am six feet tall, I can't reach the top shelf. I wonder fleetingly if previous occupants left anything up there, but dismiss going for the ladder to check it out.

As I rearrange the clutter and wipe the shelves, I am surprised by the inventory of six, count them s-i-x, bottles of hot-pepper sauce. It would seem we are inordinately fond of the fiery stuff or absent-minded in the extreme, buying yet another bottle when we can't remember if we already have one. I line them up like little red soldiers alongside a polyglot of tea tins, vinegar bottles, and small, seldom-used porcelain dishes. I choose a tin of orange pekoe and yield to the temptation to relax.

Taking a break is a classic pitfall of spring cleaning. We brew tea, sit down to smell the fine air, and notice that dazzling sunlight. Odds are good that we will falter, but I am wary of this proclivity. After one cup of tea, I trudge to the dining room. I flick a bit of candlewax from the sideboard, and the room looks quite presentable. The living room passes the same uncompromising scrutiny.

Now it's time to go upstairs and tackle the bedroom closet, but first I must get a plastic trash bag from the kitchen pantry. There, I discover more grocery sacks than anyone could ever need. Sidetracked, I bag the bags and find the dustpan hidden under them. Backing out of the pantry, I bump an open box of pasta. Spaghetti tumbles to the floor like jackstraws. With the dustpan and a surge of irritation, I clean up the pasta. "The pantry is beyond help," I tell myself as I close the door.

My mind wanders as I plunge into the closet. We'll be going to the beach soon, and it seems prudent to search for my bathing suit that is stored somewhere in the compartment, so I'll just straighten while I rummage. I fold sweaters and put them away. In a far corner is a Christmas present I could not find last December. (Am I the only one who hides gifts too well?) And here is a cotton blanket that grew from double-bed-size to king-size. It enlarged with each washing, and I simply assigned the expanding coverlet to the king-size bed until it outgrew even that. I never found the bathing suit, but did stumble upon a shoe I'd accused the Labs of eating.

Dismissing the impenetrable mass of papers, books, and unanswered letters on my desk as too much to handle at the end of the day, I check up on my husband, who is sweeping the garage. Nearing the place, I hear the unmistakable sound of a fishing reel being turned. The floor is littered with tackle. "How's your spring cleaning coming?" I ask. "Fine," he says. "I've aired my waders, oiled this salmon reel, and sorted my dry flies. And I swept half the floor. Find your bathing suit?" "No," I answered, "but I cleaned half the closet."

Stormy Litter

A prolonged and devastating drought held summer in its searing grip. The landscape was dry, dusty, brittle, depressing. It was early September and sweltering. Kenneth was away on business, and I was "holding the fort" for the first time since I became legally blind. I was restless, edgy. It was too hot to sit on the sunporch. I glanced at myself in the hall mirror. "At least my hair is growing out," I thought, looking at my short, downy growth. The scar on my head was easily visible, but it was fading. The neurosurgeon who removed the benign tumor from my optic nerve had reassured me that this would happen. After having someone underfoot constantly, I was enjoying the solitude in spite of my restlessness; however, I was uneasy about Nikki. Our usually lean and active Labrador retriever was pregnant and due any time now. She was swollen and listless. I felt sorry about her discomfort in the oppressive heat, but I hoped she wouldn't have the puppies until my husband returned.

No such luck. Late that afternoon a light wind sprang up. The dark surface of Otter Pond, visible from the sunporch at the back of the house, swirled and eddied in the rising wind. The rhododendrons surrounding the house rustled dryly in the hot breeze. I could hear thunder growling in the distance. Just before sundown, thunderheads were forming on the horizon. The thunder kept up until bedtime, but not a drop of rain fell.

Deep in the night I jerked awake to the sound of wind whipping the curtains at the open window. A shockingly close crack and flash of lightning eerily illuminated the bedroom for an instant. Thunder boomed incessantly. "Two o'clock" shone in red letters on the bedside clock. I jumped out of bed and hurried to the windows. Light, misty rain blew against me as I reached to lower them. Through the heavy clangor of the oncoming storm I heard a high, unrelenting, heart-wrenching whine. "Nikki!" I slammed the windows, grabbed a shirt and pair of shorts, and scrambled for my deck shoes. I had promised to call my friend, Jane, when it was time for Nikki's pups to come. "No matter what time it is," Jane had insisted. Without hesitation, I dialed her number.

"It's time," I said. "I haven't been down to the kennel yet, but I can hear her, and I know it's time."

"I'll be right over," Jane said sleepily.

"Hellish storm coming." I hurried down the curving stairs, clinging to the banister. In the foyer I grabbed my cane and, instinctively, a flashlight.

I stepped off the porch into a hard, cold, driving rain. By the time I bumbled my way through the thicket, my clothes were soaked and water streamed down my face. As lightning flashed, I could see Jed, the sire of Nikki's pups, and Buie, our yellow female Lab, standing in the downpour at the gates of their kennels. They had heard me coming, and no doubt Nikki's whining and the storm had disturbed them. "It's okay," I said. "Get in your houses, Jed and Buie."

I felt my way to the back of Nikki's house. She was no longer crying, but I heard her digging at the shredded paper that I had put inside. I lifted and pushed the removable roof and shone the light inside.

"Hey, Nick," I said, reaching inside to pat her. She turned from her digging, looked up at me with glazed eyes.

"It'll be all right, girl," I said, trying to soothe her. I heard Jane's sports car spin into the gravel drive. The door slammed, and Jane, in slicker and with a flashlight and towel, came crashing through the bushes.

"Wouldn't you know!" she huffed. "Months of drought and the heavens open up for the whelping. How's she doing? Any trouble?"

"She's digging and digging," I said. Jane turned her beam into the dog house.

"She's lying down. She'll have the first one soon, I hope."

We shoved the roof back in place, but left a corner ajar so we could peep inside.

We stood in the rainstorm, softly encouraging Nikki. Before too long, the first fat, black puppy appeared. We watched. Nikki licked the puppy and turned away.

"It's not moving," I cried. "The puppy's not moving or making a sound."

Jane reached inside the house and lifted the puppy up, sheltering it with the thick towel. Low and sad, she said, "Dead."

I was suddenly overwhelmingly sad. Tears mingled with the rain on my cheeks. I couldn't answer. Jane wrapped the dead puppy in the towel and placed it aside. Finally, I got control of myself and said, "We'll have to watch closely to be sure Nikki is okay, that the next one doesn't take too long."

We didn't have long to wait. Another pup arrived shortly. Another black, shining little miniature Nikki.

"She'll be all right now," Jane said. "This puppy's fine, and the others should come quickly. Let's leave her in peace while you get into some dry clothes."

I agreed. And we made our way toward the house, the constant lightning and thunder crashing around us.

Inside, I dried off, changed clothes, and located a slicker.

"I was so excited and in such a hurry I didn't even think about the storm," I grinned. "Let's go back and see how Nikki is doing."

The rain was still coming down in torrents, but only thick streaks of lightning lit the sky. The storm seemed to be drifting away, leaving the rain in its trail. We went inside the kennel run, squatted down, and flashed light into the blackness of Nikki's house. Nikki, looking totally spent, was lying on her side with five tiny black puppies, noses to her belly, all in a row. When Nikki saw us, she summoned the energy for one thump of her tail. Jane and I, in silence, watched Nikki and her puppies for a moment, and then, as if by some silent signal, stood up, quietly closed the kennel door, and went back to the house.

The Puppy Basket

Baskets and country houses are natural companions, and old baskets are especially intriguing. It is fun to discover what an old basket was used for, who might have made it, or where it came from. Often form defines function, as in a "gizzard" or "fanny" basket. The fanny basket, with two capacious compartments separated by a deep crease, was designed to straddle a horse's neck just in front of the saddle, so that eggs could safely be carried to market. Other examples are the fisherman's creel, designed to fit snugly against the fisherman's side while keeping his catch cool, and feather baskets, often pear-shaped, with a narrow neck and wide bottom so that down feathers could be stored. The narrow neck, and a lid, minimized "floating up" of the elusive down.

The list could go on and on, and a wide swath of utility, farm, and household baskets served multiple purposes. But it's not just the matter of a basket's function. I like the feel, the heft, the shape, and smell of old baskets. Some are rough, simply made. Others are finely woven and finished. I like to hold the handmade handles and wonder how many others have used the basket. I wonder who grew the special willow, or who walked into the forest to cut the tree to be used for the splits, or weavers. I like to imagine the basketmaker weaving and shaping the natural materials into a basket that is uniquely his or hers. In a way, every old basket carries the fingerprints of its maker, and traces of the persons who have used it. I once bought an old fish basket on the coast of North Carolina. It was a round basket woven with an open, hexagonal design. The handle was hand-cut and wrapped with fine reed. I could imagine a woman walking to the docks when the fishing boats came in from the sea, and choosing the fish she would cook for supper. When her basket was full, she might dip it in the salt water to rinse and refresh the fish. Then she'd walk home with her basket of fresh fish, still dripping from the sea. The basket, when I bought it, was silvery gray with hints of iridescence caused by salt and seawater. Almost every basket stirs my imagination. And I always use them.

At an auction many years ago, I successfully bid on a splint basket. It was rectangular, almost a yard long and about ten inches deep. It was well made, sturdy, a rich tan. It had a firmly wrapped top rim with insert grips at each end. I bought it for a super-sized picnic basket or for storing and toting whatever needs storing and toting. It went on many a picnic in the country and tailgate parties. I'd line it with a gingham cloth and fill it with containers of picnic fixings. It could hold everything needed for a fried chicken–potato salad–sand-wiches type picnic. It was a very handy basket.

When Nikki's puppies started tumbling around and were big enough to be handled, petted, and played with, the picnic basket became "the puppy basket," and that is the name it has retained. Kenneth would load the wiggling pups in the basket, and with Nikki right on his heel, bring the basket full of puppies to the sunporch. The sunporch had a brick floor, which we covered with newspapers. (It could also be hosed off.)

When the puppies and Nikki were brought inside, it was the "happy hour." Nikki seemed happy for a little break from her always-hungry offspring, the puppies were happy to explore the new territory, and we were happy to fool with the puppies. Friends and houseguests loved the happy hour with the puppies. I've never met anyone who didn't warm up to a puppy. It is no surprise to me that dogs, cats, and other pets are being used today to cheer the elderly and the ill in convalescent homes, and in therapy to reach patients who have previously been unreachable. Anytime I was feeling gloomy, a visit with the puppies was a sure cure.

In the beginning, the five little pups would huddle in the basket until they were lifted out and placed on the floor. They wouldn't be on the floor long before someone would find a puppy irresistible and pick it up. The pudgy, jet-black pups would waddle off in all directions. In time, they'd come when called, unless distracted by another puppy who wanted to play. It was startling to hear such small creatures bark so sharply.

As the puppies grew, they'd stand on their hind legs and look over the side of the basket when being toted to the sunporch. Kenneth tried to keep them down in the basket, for fear they'd tumble over the side, but it was an impossible job. There never was an accident, as the puppies seemed to understand that the ride in the basket was temporary. The instant Kenneth set it on the floor, they'd try to scramble over the side.

By the time they were eight weeks old, the puppies were a heavy load in the puppy basket. And they were a heart-warming sight: healthy, curious, fat, and clumsy, with feet that seemed too big for their bodies, floppy eared and endearingly friendly. The two females and the three males were a basketful, a handful, and it was time to let them go. But letting them go, even to excellent homes, was tearful business. Tears were shed over each puppy that was taken away by a happy new owner. I have the basket still. And I wonder if some day, when I am gone and someone else takes the basket home, they will ever imagine that it is, for all time, a puppy basket.

Knee Deep in Summer

On a languorous summer day when the sweet scent of strawberries and flowered fields fills the air, sit in a porch rocker and consider the poet's intent. Sometimes summer, that rich and glorious season, is lost between compulsive activity and total lethargy. It slips by; and we wonder where it went, how we squandered the days.

This is a time when we could learn from our ancestors. Though hardworking, they also knew the value of relaxation, of being neither the grasshopper nor the ant. Balance is the key. Just look at what they bequeathed us for the happy pursuit of restorative pleasures.

The rocking chair. Oldfangled or newfangled, the rocker continues in its ageless tasks of comforting fretting infants, soothing tired bodies, delighting energetic children—just by providing a haven for sitting and rocking.

Put the rocker on a porch, and the simple pleasure of rocking is intensified by the summer fragrances, the sounds of nature. Our grandparents knew the delight of a country porch in summer—their houses nearly always had at least one; some were surrounded by porches.

The unrestricted feeling of a porch, even one with a limited vista, is remarkable and relaxing. It is a fine place to go with a friend, or with a book and grandmother's pressed-glass pitcher full of lemon-ade. Doing needlework, writing letters, shelling beans, even peeling onions becomes more enjoyable in the open air. The romantic, so-ciable aspects of the porch endure.

As we pause to appreciate summer, we may be lucky enough to be pausing in a swing—on the porch, or in a pleasant spot in the yard. Our forefathers designed swings sensibly: open-armed, slatted, two-seated benches with the back slanted at a comfortable angle. If on the porch, they were hung on chains or stout rope; outside, they were suspended under a shade tree or from a cross beam between two posts.

As children, we never gave up the joy of a simple swing hung from a tree limb, never stopped trying to touch the sky with our toes. As adults, always hurrying, we ignored the swing, relegating it to the realm of the idle. But happily, it is making a comeback. Someone has rediscovered its virtues, judging by the handsomely designed swings now available. Some are lucky enough to find one stashed away in the attic or barn. So, take time to enjoy its soothing comfort.

The hammock, a swing's first cousin, requires a little caution in order to achieve comfort. On entering one, you may be dumped un-ceremoniously on the ground. But whether made of bright canvas or strong twine, a hammock strung between two trees beside the garden path is a good friend when the basket of tomatoes grows heavy. Set the basket down and cool off a minute before going on to the kitchen with your load. Stretch out and look at the blue of the sky. However, be prepared to be joined by a few mosquitoes and gnats, who love finding an occupied hammock. Offset this with another simple coun-try pleasure—fanning with a broad-brimmed straw hat.

No aspect of the good and simple life was neglected by our ancestors. Fun was provided with the invention of the ice-cream freezer. Anyone who has taken part in the unforgettable ritual of homemade ice cream will swear to this. The mixture of cream, milk, sugar, and fresh fruit was poured into a metal cylinder (usually one-quart size), then a paddle-type "dasher" was fitted into the middle and the lid put on. After the cylinder was set into the "freezer" (a large wooden bucket), a handle was attached and clamped securely to the rim. Crushed ice and rock salt were packed around the container and the cranking began.

At first the container would spin freely, but the job became more difficult as the ice cream hardened. When the lid was finally taken off, there was a mad scramble among the children wanting to "lick the dasher" after it was removed from the ice cream.

The wholesome, delicate flavor of homemade ice cream has no substitute on a hot summer day. This simple pleasure is still ours. The fun of the hand-cranked freezer can be replaced by the convenience of the electric ice–cream maker. One summer a few years ago, I bought an electric one at a garage sale and took it to the beach with us. Its busy whirr was heard constantly on our back deck, delighting everybody—especially the droves of teenagers. After a blistering day on the sand, cones of homemade ice cream were always in demand.

So here we are, knee deep in summer, taking it all in, aware of the gentle reminders from the past that time is fleeting. Perhaps somewhere among our busyness we can take heed from Shakespeare and "by indirection find direction." Maybe tomorrow we'll have breakfast on the porch.

October Magic

When tangled bittersweet brightened the hedgerows where my husband, Kenneth, hunted pheasant, he often came home with a bouquet of the orange-berried vine mixed with cattails, teasel, dried sedge, and milkweed. I arranged the woodland offering in a brown-glazed crock, sometimes adding a few colorful feathers from the pheasants.

October was filled with a multitude of pleasures for Kenneth. Perhaps we are always partial to the month in which we were born, but his affection for it went far beyond simple preference. The period increased his energy, enthusiasm, and good humor. He loved the season's splendid colors and the richness of the fall crops. He collected materials from the woods along with bunches of red, yellow, burgundy, and russet leaves. These arrangements soon turned brown, but they stood in a vase on the hearth or table while in their glory. He also carried home autumn squash, string bags of super-size onions, Indian corn, and, always, pumpkins.

We hung the multicolored corn on the door and set the pumpkins on the steps in tribute to the beautiful season. When our grandson lived with us, the pumpkins were stacked three deep at every entrance to the house.

Kenneth's love of October is shared by people everywhere who are astonished by the month's enduring beauty and its brisk, invigorating weather. Kenneth loved the outdoors, and when the first sunny, crisp days dawned, he rose early. He rattled logs at the woodpile, brought them inside, dropped them noisily on the hearth, and then went about one of our favorite pleasures—building a crackling fire. Wood smoke in the air sent Kenneth to the bookshelves to pick out favorite volumes, many of them sporting books at this time of the year. When time allows one to sit by the fire and read, nothing is more comforting than books stacked handily within reach. During our years together, we shared many wonderful fireside hours.

As the weather transformed field and forest so beautifully, Kenneth's mind was busy choosing among the delights of pursuing fast-flying woodcock in the swales where alders grew, taking one of the Labs to hunt pheasant, admiring the woodpile, or picking up apples in the backyard while considering the possibility of surf casting on the Outer Banks of our home state, North Carolina.

October also meant a heightened interest in cooking and socializing with friends. For a man who detested casseroles, Kenneth, paradoxically, enjoyed classic cassoulet of game, sausage, and beans. We would often prepare the dish together, inevitably squabbling over how much garlic or thyme to add or how to slice the sausages. (My husband was a powerful and worthy adversary on any point of discussion. You had to stand your ground on any point, especially if you felt strongly about how much garlic to use.) He would ladle the savory mixture onto the plates, pass them to friends at the table, and sniff appreciatively.

Spaghetti was another dish we frequently wrangled over. We agreed on the preparation of meatballs and sauce but went to war over whether or not to rinse the al dente pasta. We never settled the dispute, but we enjoyed serving Italian food to houseguests on October weekends.

The pleasures of travel seem magnified in the fine autumn weather. Kenneth and I loved to take trips together: Our journeys could be as close as the back roads of the nearby provinces or as far-flung as the European countryside. We were lucky enough to see red grouse on the Highland moors, play golf on a windy day at St. Andrews in Scotland, picnic on wine and cheese beside the Loire in France, and visit such countries as Germany, England, Wales, and Italy.

Yes. October is a fine time for all of us to go for a walk through the fallen leaves with our dogs and, of course, to rake the yard. We take time to lean on the rake and smell the woodsy air. We renew friendships, enjoy family, share books, dream by the fire, and put extra quilts in the bedroom. We pause and admire the woodland bouquet brought with love.

The season also awakens remembrances. I will never forget one afternoon when Kenneth and I sat together on a small balcony overlooking the harbor at Portofino, Italy. Little boats at anchor were reflected in the calm sea, and the voices of two boys playing with a cat on a harborside dock rose clearly through the cool air. The name of the small hotel, Splendido, will always remind me of October days we spent together. If, as Kenneth often said, "life is a series of memories," then this October I'll recall the happy times we shared.

An Unforgettable English Christmas

The week before Christmas, Kenneth and I were settled by the fireplace in our small country library, having a predinner drink while we watched the evening news. The fire sputtered softly, a comforting sound that contrasted with the cold, gusty wind that caused the big window in the library to sweat, as though in fear. When the weatherman came on, the forecast for Christmas week was grim, unless you were a skier who relished gliding down icy slopes clad in a fortune of goosedown-insulated clothing. "Bitter cold and snow," Kenneth repeated after the weatherman.

"I'm glad this is one year we're staying home and not having company," he said. "I'd hate for the kids to travel in this kind of weather." I agreed. "It will be nice to spend Christmas here," I said. I rose, turned the TV off, and returned to my chair. Tar and Nikki, our Labrador retrievers, were sprawled out at our feet, gently snoring after an afternoon run in the light snow at the nearby hunt club.

We had only recently started living full-time in the stone farmhouse, and we were looking forward to a quiet, uncomplicated Christmas. "Let's have something simple for Christmas dinner." "That's fine with me," Kenneth answered. "How would you like a steak grilled over coals in the fireplace?" "Fine!" I sighed. "Speaking of dinner, we'd better eat, or we'll both doze off in front of the fire. But I'll serve our plates and bring in two trays, OK?" "Good idea," Kenneth nodded, getting up to throw a log on the fire. And then the phone rang, jangling the quiet. I stepped to the next room to answer it. The telephone stood on a polished walnut board that covered a long, low, old-fashioned radiator in the dining room. Poo, our hefty orange tabby, was curled in his favorite warm spot, undisturbed by the ringing telephone.

The unmistakable, lilting English accent of Alison Harrison came through the receiver. "Jo," she chimed, "Malcolm and I have a splendid idea—we're going to have a traditional English feast this Christmas Day, and we would love it if you and Kenny would celebrate with us. We're having other friends from the university. We'll be coming to the country with the children Christmas Eve, and our other guests will follow. We're planning to have roast suckling pig with brandy stuffing, and all the trimmings, including a proper plum pudding, and trifle as well!" she said, warming to her traditions. "We put coins and other trinkets in the trifle, you know—it's fun as well as being delicious. Do say you'll join us." "It sounds wonderful," I replied somewhat hesitantly, considering the quiet holiday Kenneth and I had been talking about. "I don't mean to be rude, but would you excuse me a moment while I tell Kenny about your delightful invitation?" I hurried into the library. Kenneth had overheard my end of the conversation. "Who is it?" he asked, in a loud whisper. "It's Alison," I said. "They want us to come to their place Christmas Day for a traditional English dinner. Roast suckling pig." Kenneth sat up abruptly, quick to pick up on something new and fun. "Alison and

Malcolm," he said in a voice that could have been heard at the barn outside. "We'll be there with sleigh bells on!" The truth was, we liked Malcolm and Alison very much, and we'd have accepted no matter what they were serving. It wouldn't be a quiet dinner together by the fire, but a festive English dinner with friends in their old farmhouse down the road. When I picked up the receiver again, I said to Alison, "Surely you heard that. Any further acceptance needed?" "None," she replied, "see you Christmas."

As Christmas drew closer, we were busy with last-minute shopping and decorating. Kenneth brought two big bunches of mistletoe from the woods at the hunt club. He hung one bunch over the back door—where everyone came in. "I'll tie a red bow on the other bunch and we'll take it to Alison and Malcolm on Christmas, along with the bottles of wine that I've already packed in a gift basket." Kenneth busied himself splitting kindling while I fussed with finishing touches on the tree—an amended version of our usual heavily decorated evergreen. Since we were to be alone, we had decorated it with enough ornaments to please us but not with the usual full regalia. We were simplifying things this relaxed holiday.

Christmas Eve dawned with an ominous mackerel sky. "Looks like we're in for snow," Kenneth said, studying the fish-scale pattern of the clouds through the library window. He had already built a fire in the fireplace, and we had taken our morning coffee in to read the papers. "Turn on the TV and maybe we can catch the weather report," I suggested. "I don't need to hear the report," he said. "It's going to snow any time. And the Harrisons will have a hell of a time getting up that driveway of theirs."

Malcolm and Alison and their three children, Joanne, Simon, and Eve, only came to the country on weekends and holidays. They were restoring a rambling century-old farmhouse that sat on a bluff that rose sharply from the highway. Their house, like ours, was built conveniently next to a two-lane dirt road, with a stepping stone  where riders could dismount, and carriage passengers could get out easily and come up the stone steps to the narrow front yard. The bluff on which their house stood was at the arc of a long, downhill curve on the now busy highway. When exiting their drive, the bluff blocked the driver's view on the uphill side. To add to the difficulty, the driveway was steeply inclined from the highway to the backyard. It was one car wide, and the dirt and slag were deeply rutted. It was slick when it rained, snowed, or sleeted. Paving the driveway and grading the bluff that obscured the uphill view were among those endless improvements awaiting the restorers of the elderly homestead. Malcolm and Alison were doing as much of the work themselves as they could. They had removed walls that hid a handsome brick fireplace that, when checked for safety, worked as well as the day it was built. They had taken down unattractive ceilings to reveal original beams. The living and dining rooms were in a state of semirepair, but quite comfortable with a hardwood fire in the fireplace. They had tackled the kitchen first, and built a slate patio at the back door. Malcolm installed a big window over the new sink, and set an oven in an unused brick chimney. A careful and meticulous craftsman, he built their butcher-block counters himself, painstakingly fitting and gluing the pieces together. Their finished kitchen was cozy, bright, efficient, and comfortable. They would have no trouble producing an English feast in that setting.

"Did you hear me?" Kenneth asked. "I was saying that I expect the Harrisons will have trouble getting in their driveway." "Maybe not," I said. "They have an agreement with the snowplow people to keep the drive plowed. And someone checks the place and increases the heat when the temperature drops below a certain point." "Well, that's good," Kenneth said. "I was thinking I'd better call and tell them to come early, because I feel sure we're in for really heavy snow. It's getting colder every hour. And look at that sky." The sky was bleak, darkening from fish-scale silvery gray to a deep, steely, gun-barrel gray. "Maybe they'll leave the city early," I said. "Surely they didn't have classes at NYU today."

Malcolm was a professor at the university, and Alison was study-ing for a master's degree in psychology. It seemed as though we had known them for years, because we were so congenial, but actually they were friends of relatively short acquaintance. Other friends who lived across the road from the Harrisons introduced us. No matter—sooner or later we'd have met at the local hardware store—mecca for everyone involved in the endless vagaries and complexities of restor-ing an old house.

The evening sun seemed to plunge below the horizon, and the temperature plunged with it. The flurries that had danced in the wind all day steadied into thick snowfall. We turned the lights on at the back door, and the snowflakes were thick and beautiful, like a lace curtain shifting in the wind. "It's 20 degrees already," Kenneth said. "It'll be in the teens before midnight. The roads will be murder." Like a duplicate picture of the night Alison called, we were watching the news in the library, bolstering ourselves against the cold with a toddy. Tar and Nikki were in front of the fire. Poo, who had no fear of the Labs, was between them, stretched out just like the dogs. Once more—the telephone rang. Kenneth was poking at the fire. "That apple wood smells good," he said, turning a log over, producing a shower of sparks. "I'll get it," I said over my shoulder, already halfway to the insistently ringing phone. "Hello?" It was Alison, sounding uncharacteristically upset, her usually cheerful voice edged with anxiety. "What a terrible time we're having. It's an awful mess." I could hear Eve, their youngest child, crying. "What in the world is happening?" I asked, alarmed. Hearing me, Kenneth came in to see what was going on. Alison said, "Malcolm is out talking to the police. There was an accident in front of our house. Not us. The plumbers." Her words came out in a torrent, bumping into one another. "Alison, calm down," I said. "Tell me exactly what happened." "Eve, it's going to be fine. Keep quiet for a moment," I heard her comforting the child in a sharp voice. Her efforts did not help.

After a brief silence, the child set in again, and Alison spoke into the receiver, less edgy. "First of all, when we arrived, the driveway was half covered with snow, but Malcolm gunned the car and we shot up the driveway like a drunk snake, skidding from side to side. We all bailed out of the car and hurried to the back door through the snow. When we stepped in the kitchen, it was ice cold. Simon was the first in, running as usual, and when his feet hit the floor, he skidded halfway across the kitchen and bumped into a chair. There's a slick of ice all over the kitchen floor. The person who checks on the house must have come early today, before the temperature dropped. The whole place is as cold as a tomb; the furnace won't work; pipes have burst in the walls, flooding the place; and we have an ice skating rink in the living room, much thicker than the one in the kitchen." "Good Lord," was all I could manage. Alison continued, some of her characteristic humor returning. "If it weren't so bad, it would be fun," she said, choking back a laugh. "What about the police there?" I asked. "Well," she said, "the first thing we did was build a fire and heat water. The children are taking turns clutching a water bottle under the blankets they're wrapped in. Once we were sure the kids were okay, we called plumbers. I had no idea we'd find them available on Christmas Eve, but they answered—rather more cheerfully than you'd expect on a holiday. As Malcolm told them what was wrong out here, he was astonished when they very happily agreed to come out at once. They knew the house because they'd done work for us before. When they came roaring up the icy driveway and slid into the large cedar in the backyard, we were not unduly alarmed. But when Malcolm opened the kitchen door to let them in, it was clear they were so agreeable because they were full of Christmas spirits. They wobbled in, one carrying a large toolbox, which he dropped as he lost his balance on the icy floor. We caught him in mid-flight and stood him up. I thought

Malcolm might bean them with one of the wrenches that slid across the floor, but he simply glared at them, muttering 'merry hell, merry hell.'

Kenneth was at my elbow. "What's *wrong?*" he insisted. Turning from the phone, I said, "It's Alison. The pipes have burst. Wait a minute, will you, while she finishes telling me!" I shot back grouchily. Alison went on, ignoring our domestic skirmish. "The plumbers went down in the cellar with Malcolm right behind them. I could hear them stumbling on the stairs. Then I heard all this clanging, as though they were beating on the pipes. Then Malcolm came back and said, 'They're drunk as loons. And of course—they don't have the right tools.' He didn't think they could fix anything if they had every wrench in Warwick. They wanted to go get the tools they needed, but it was hopeless, so he told them to forget it and go home."

I waited for her to continue, Kenneth irritatedly pacing the floor. "Malcolm told them to drive carefully, and that he would stand on the uphill slope and signal them when the road was clear. He carried a flashlight to signal with. He was waiting for a car to go past on the highway before waving them out the driveway, and they backed out the driveway without looking. A Volkswagen was coming down the road and skidded into them, broadside. The plumbers were fine, but the driver of the VW has a hurt foot. The plumbers wanted to drive the injured man to the doctor! Malcolm shouted at them to stay out of the road and ran in here and called the police. They're out there helping the man out of the VW and getting ready to take him to the hospital to be sure he's okay, and I don't know what they're saying to the plumbers. Our guests will be coming any minute and there's a wreck in our driveway." As she paused disconsolately, I said, "Alison, you all must come down here." Kenneth grabbed the phone and in his best executive voice commanded, "Alison, you and Malcolm and the children come on down here as soon as you can. Bring your friends. We'll have your English Christmas right here." "Thank you," she said. Kenneth placed the receiver in its cradle, a look of alarm spread over his face. "Hell!" he said, "I think she was about to cry." Looking away from me, he muttered, "It's a good thing I stacked extra wood on the porch." He pulled his down hunting jacket off the peg in the back entry, sat down, shucked off his warm slippers, and slid his feet into snow boots and laced them up. He put on the jacket, a hat, and gloves. "Alison said they'd be along very soon, because their friends were leaving only a short time after they did. They should be arriving right away."

I could hear him shoveling the short walk from our kitchen door to the driveway. He had a very short wait. He'd barely finished shoveling when two cars turned in our driveway, their headlights blurry in the snowfall. I had my boots and warm clothes on by then, and stood beside him, waiting for our friends. "Wonder how many kids there will be?" he said. "Six," I answered, as children and adults came tromping through the snow to the path. "Come in, introductions inside."

When everyone was inside, the children dashed for the fire, followed by the retrievers, who had greeted everyone with decorations off the tree in their mouths. Both the dogs had snatched glass balls off the lower branches, and Kenneth hurried to take them from the dogs. Retrievers are like that—when anyone comes to the door, friend or foe, the dogs will have something in their mouths—dish cloth, boot, anything handy.

The Harrisons' friends were Jim, a physician; his wife, Gail; and their children, Jimmy, Melissa, and Amy. Kenneth and I were having oyster stew for dinner, so we stretched it a bit and filled a platter with a heap of cold roast beef sandwiches and a few peanut butter-and-jellies thrown in for good measure. Everyone was apologetic about barging in, but there was no way to get back to the city in this weather. We assured them that we were happy to have them, and quieted their apologies by asking them if they wouldn't help us if we were in the same situation. After that, everyone settled in. The men built an additional fire in the living room, so everyone could gather by the hearth. The dogs were half crazy with the excitement of having children in the house and a dozen people willing to give them a pat. Poo, less enthusiastic about this invasion of his quiet territory, took refuge on top of a tall bookcase, where he crouched and stared down at the throng.

After drinks and cheese and crackers by the fire, we all sat down to eat, children at a portable table in the living room, adults at the dining room table. Kenneth opened wine, and it was a very nice Christmas Eve dinner, even if improvised. We sat in the glow of the sparsely decorated Christmas tree, able to laugh about the situation. But we needed to get the children to bed. They were keyed up and afraid that Santa Claus would not find them in this strange place. Amy solemnly tugged at her father's coat sleeve and said, "Maybe we could call the North Pole and tell him where we are." We all suppressed our laughter, but were unable to hide our smiles as Jim told all the children (with the believability of all doctors) that "Santa Claus knows where good little boys and girls are at all times. It is mysterious, and we are not certain how he knows, but we must believe it—because he knows, and he will bring your gifts here." With that, we ushered the children to their appointed sleeping quarters. We had four bedrooms, so the logistics were complicated. We had to put all the children upstairs so that St. Nicholas would not be discovered bringing the toys and gifts downstairs. So, the two older girls shared one bedroom, and Eve and Amy were to share their parents' bedrooms. The little girls were delighted with this privilege, and went to bed without too much encouragement, pacified by having a light left on in their rooms. I also noticed they each took a teddy bear to bed. "Wise," I thought, "never know when you'll need a hug in the dark." We dragged a spare mattress out of the walk-in attic, and placed it on the floor in Kenneth's gun room, which was next to our bedroom, which was to be occupied by Alison and Malcolm. The mattress was outfitted with quilts and pillows, and the boys would be quite comfortable. Kenneth made certain the gun cabinets were locked. Kenneth's snoring was notorious, so there were no serious objections when we said we'd sleep on a pallet in the library.

Finally, the children were asleep, and St. Nick set to work. Malcolm and Jim had to go back to the Harrison's house to bring presents that had been hidden there weeks before. Kenneth took them in our Jeep. It was still snowing heavily, deepening on the ground, as we brought packages in from the two cars. The path was snowed over and slippery. It was beautiful and still, no traffic on the road. The pile of gifts under the tree reached the lowest branches and fanned out in a big circle. A Raggedy Ann sat in a small doll's chair, and a fly rod was propped near the tree. (That was for Simon, a young but ardent angler.) After the gifts were in, we came to the provisions that Alison had brought for the English feast. I picked up a carefully wrapped bundle, and was surprised at its weight. "What is this heavy thing?" I asked. Casting a glance at it as I dropped it on the kitchen counter, she said, "The pig."

The suckling pig, bundled in a thick swaddling of butcher's paper, would not fit in the fridge. But we couldn't leave it outside, or it would freeze. We were interrupted by the sound of the Jeep chugging in the driveway. The men came in, shivering and stamping snow off their boots. Shedding boots and heavy clothes, Malcolm said, "Pour us a drink while we haul in the entire F.A.O. Schwartz." When the remainder of the toys and gifts were under the tree, someone commented that they were relieved there were no bikes or tricycles to assemble. Then we came back to the problem of refrigerating the pig overnight. We all went to the kitchen. "Cut it in half," said the doctor. "I don't care what you do with it," said the professor, "I'm burned out on crises, major and minor." He picked up his drink, and we could hear a sigh of relief as he sank into a comfortable chair. The publisher (Kenneth) suggested, "Take off the cover and make it a smaller package." We did so, but it did nothing to decrease the length of the pig, which was the problem. We all stood looking at the plump, white carcass with the short snout and floppy ears. For a moment I got a lump in my throat. "Maybe I'll have a sip of your drink," I said to Kenneth, reaching for his glass and taking a big gulp. He looked at me in astonishment. I hate Scotch. Then his gaze fell on the pig.

"Hmm. Tell you what, put it in a plastic bag." He went to the refrigerator, rearranged some of its contents, and lowered the top shelf. "Let me have the pig," he said, like a man who knows he has to carry a land mine a short distance. The only size bag we had would not quite cover the little porker. Kenneth thrust the bag and contents into the refrigerator, positioning the pig on its haunches. The plastic bag slid down, exposing the pig. "Get some string," Kenneth said, as desperate as a man crying for a lifeline. He tied the sack just below the pig's head—creating the effect of a pig with a ruff around its neck. He propped the sitting pig up with a gallon jug of milk and a gallon of orange juice. He slammed the door and demanded, "Where's my drink?"

We had to rouse Malcolm, who was asleep in the chair. "I'm exhausted," he said, heading for the stairs. When everyone had gone upstairs, Kenneth and I arranged a pile of quilts on the floor in front of the fire in the library. It was comfortable enough. His head resting on his folded arms, Kenneth looked out the window. "Still snowing," he said. "I'm worn out." "Me, too. And I don't know how we'll cook that long pig." We went to sleep before the last flickering light of the fire.

It seemed we had only dozed off when we were jolted awake by a scream from the kitchen. It was daylight. The dogs, next to us in the night, jumped up and ran, barking, to the kitchen. Kenneth jumped up, grabbed his pants, and hopped into them. "My back's killing me," he said as he stumbled toward the kitchen. I followed him, half awake. So did everyone else in the house. Even Poo came in and hopped up on the kitchen counter, tail erect. Joanne stood beside the open refrigerator door, an empty glass in her hand. When we all clustered around her, she pointed, transfixed, at the pig sitting behind the milk and juice. "What is that?" Her voice quavered. "It's grinning at me. It's awful." Kenneth said, "It's a pig in a poke." So our movable English feast began with the terrified scream of a girl who tiptoed into the kitchen for a glass of orange juice.

There could have been no finer diversion than presents and toys under the tree. The snow had stopped, but it stood in deep drifts, and evergreens were bent with their heavy white coating. The sun was out, and the surrounding landscape shone and glittered in the light. "We certainly have a white Christmas," Gail said, raising her voice above the clamor of the children opening packages. When the mountain of crumpled wrapping paper was picked up and the children were occupied with their treasures, the adults exchanged gifts.

We were all in splendid humor as we offered to lend Alison a hand with preparations for our English feast. She had already made brandy stuffing for the pig, and we watched as she expertly trussed it. The plum pudding was aged, the trifle was made, and all the vegetables and trimmings were in order. Alison placed the pig on a rack in the largest pan from my cupboard. She opened the preheated oven, inserted the pan, and the rear extremity of the pig stuck out over the pan and beyond the oven shelf. There was a thoughtful silence. "Malcolm!" Alison called, keeping her voice calm. "Come here, please."

The upshot was that Malcolm had foreseen this possibility and had come prepared. He extracted what looked like an Erector set from his baggage, cleared the things from a table in the living room, and calmly sat down and began constructing a spit. He even had the elec-

tric motor to turn it. Kenneth shook his head in disbelief as Malcolm
tinkered unhurriedly at his project. It was getting later and later, and
we exchanged nervous glances, mentally calculating how long it would
take to roast a Christmas pig, too long for the oven, on a homemade
spit in a fireplace. The eggnog was soon dispensed with, and a sullen
silence set in, broken occasionally by a skirmish among the children
or a dispute between the dogs over fallen bits of Christmas candy and
cookies.

When the construction of the spit was finally completed, we all
cheered. The pig was balanced on the spit, and the motor turned on.
It rotated smartly. Too smartly. As efficiently as an engineer on a train,
Malcolm quickly slowed down the revolutions of the spit, just before
it looked like the spinning dervish would fling the pig into the living
room. The dogs, not unintelligent, were standing by in case this should
come to pass. We all calmed down, accepting the fact that we might
not have our Christmas feast until New Year's Day. The pig revolved
with a hypnotizing motion and sound, and we chatted and watched.
The clock ticked on and on. The suckling pig had advanced from a
rosy pink to a light golden brown. Malcolm, wishing to speed things
up, had constructed an aluminum foil shield to fit inside the fireplace
to reflect the heat toward the steadily turning pig. From time to time,
adjustments would be made to ensure that the main course remained
in balance on the spit. At this point, an alarming thing happened.
The brandy stuffing, warmed by the fire, became very liquid, and
began seeping out of openings in the piggy. "Look at that!" squealed
Jimmy. "It's going to the bathroom!" The children came closer, snick-
ering and complaining. "I'm not eating *that* thing," was the consen-

sus of the younger crowd. "*Quiet!*" Malcolm roared, stuffing wads of aluminum foil into the openings, as deftly as a surgeon. "Well done," cheered Jim, lifting his glass. The physician had dealt with the tedium of waiting for the feast by making numerous trips to the pantry, wherein the spirits were. "Jolly well done!" he added.

The children had had candy and cookies and other snacks, but it was getting on toward dinner time. "I'm hungry," one said, and the wail was taken up as a chorus. "How about hamburgers?" I asked. "Yea!" was the collective response. "Got any fries?" Kenneth chimed in. "Fix some extras, we might all have a burger while we wait for the entré."

As the pig turned and the world turned, and the sun went down on the deep snow, we sat around the fire, eating our hamburgers and sharing a big bowl of French fries. The delicious smell of roasting pork filled the house. It was clear that the suckling pig was far from being done, but brainstorming brought up that it had reduced in size, and perhaps it would now fit into the oven. So the pig was carefully slipped off the spit and into the roasting pan. Same result. Still too long for the oven. So Alison and I, wearing insulated mitts, held the forelegs and the hind legs of the pig together, bending it into a U shape. Gail tied the legs together with string. We removed the rack from the pan and laid the pig in the bottom of the pan. We put the pan in the oven, and smugly closed the oven door. We went to the dining room, where everyone else was busily devouring the plum pudding and trifle. "Cheats!" I said, swiping a dab of the disappearing plum pudding. After every spoonful of dessert was gone, and the silver threepence and other trinkets had been claimed, the children wearily agreed to go to bed. It had been a long day, and the pig still wasn't done.

As we sat by the fire enjoying coffee, there was a loud *Thump*! in the kitchen. I went to the oven and looked inside. Alison was close behind me. She looked tiredly at the pig. The strings had broken loose, and the loud thump we had heard was the sound of forelegs and hind legs striking the sides of the oven. "What an unmitigated disaster," she said softly, near tears. "Are you kidding?" I said, slamming the oven door. "We haven't had this much excitement at Christmas in years. And look at the fun we've had. Everybody's full of good cheer, hamburgers, and plum pudding and trifle. Not bad, I'd say." "You're right. We'll have roast suckling pig for dessert." And we did. Complete with a crabapple in its mouth. As we sat down at the table and looked at the crispy suckling pig, presented beautifully on a platter, Malcolm carved and served each a tidbit. It was delicious, but we were all full of hamburgers and English desserts. Alison said, "Give the remainder to the Labs. And Poo. They've waited patiently all day for a treat." Kenneth, who had quietly slipped out to the pantry, came in with a tray and passed champagne glasses around. He popped the corks, and when everyone's glass was filled, he raised his to propose a toast. Standing in front of the twinkling tree, he said, "To Alison and Malcolm, who planned to share the companionship of their family and friends with us, and who wished to share a typical English Christmas with us. As far as I know they have done so admirably. It has been an unforgettable English Christmas. Please invite us again!"

THE SPORTING LIFE

W e traveled past openings in the woods where
ferns were as verdant as in a rain forest.
Where sunlight came through the trees,
brilliantly colored wildflowers turned the shoreline into an impressionistic painting.
Butterflies fluttered among the lavender,
yellow, magenta, and white flowers.
If our canoe was moving swiftly, and I squinted
into the sun, the flowers became a ribbonlike blur
of color, like ornamentation on the deep-green
wilderness. Having the river and the wilderness
to ourselves was lonely in a very touching,
romantic way. It was odd how the density of the
woods seemed to isolate and magnify each strain
of birdsong. To hear a bird sing out clearly and
brilliantly when the only sound was that of the
canoes moving steadily downstream
was as thrilling as a splendid aria.
When there is enough silence, we hear things
more clearly.

Miramichi Float Trip

I've never forgotten losing my diary of five incredibly beautiful days on the Miramichi, when Kenneth introduced me to one of his great passions, fly-fishing for Atlantic salmon. The loss was as poignant as if I'd lost a love letter. It was lost, no doubt, in one of our moves, when a book can be easily overlooked. Even so, brilliant fragments spiral through the mist of memory: the flash of sunlight on a silver salmon, the sound of rapids, the smell of a campfire, moon rise and starlight, and a resurgence of intense joy.

Before we went to New Brunswick, Canada, for our float trip on the Main Southwest branch of the Miramichi, Kenneth coached me on the matter of fly-fishing. He placed an Orvis fly rod in my hand, and at the small farm pond, I practiced casting as he counted one, two, three! It was so easy and graceful when he cast. I was awkward at first, but Kenneth badgered, encouraged, and praised. He was a persistent instructor, and I began to get the feel of it, the lift, the pause, the line shooting forward. Then we moved on to letting out line, reeling in, and lifting it off the water again. I never achieved the grace of an experienced fly fisherman, but I grew to have tremendous respect for fly-fishing, and an appreciation of the sport. Kenneth said to me, "You will love salmon fishing, and you will love the river." He was right.

"Pack light, Jo," Kenneth warned when we were getting ready for the drive to Canada. "Besides clothing and fishing gear, we'll be carrying five days' supplies in the canoes. Take just what you need. Don't forget a sweater or a fishing jacket. Even though it's July, evenings by the river are cool."

"What about rain gear?" I asked.

"I'll pack that. And our tackle. You just pack your essentials," Kenneth said.

I remember that the trip from New York was fun in spite of the long drive. With rod cases and duffles in the wagon, we took our time. We spent one night at an old-fashioned tourist court in New Hampshire. It was an attractive place. Cabins were tucked among a stand of pines. Our one-room-and-bath cabin was freshly painted white outside, and was spotlessly clean and comfortable. The small, screened front porch provided a view of a wooded hillside. There were lawn chairs under the pines beside the cabin, so we relaxed there with an evening drink, glad the long day's drive was over. The air was cool and spicily resinous. Later we ate homemade beef pot pie at a local restaurant. We slept soundly that night under a light wool blanket, with the windows open, and the soft scent of pine filling the cabin.

Next day we were on the road early, and stopped for lunch in Maine. We had steamed lobsters out on a sunny dock. Seagulls circled overhead. A few stood on the dock's rail, hoping for a tidbit. We had a leisurely lunch in the sun, enjoying the view of village houses that edged the bay, and talked of our fishing adventure. I was as excited about the trip as a kid going to the circus. From there, we moved on to L. L. Bean, a mecca for outdoor folk, where we made a quick foray for a few items before heading to the Canadian border.

I remember crossing the border, eventually driving along the St. John's River and onward, to Boiestown. My lost journal could tell me the name of the camp and the proprietor, who was the outfitter of our float trip. Alas, memory fades. I do recall the spare cabin where we spent the night, and the friendliness of everyone at the fish camp. And that the outfitter, who was retiring after many years, spoke beautifully and somewhat sadly of his time on the river.

Very early the next morning, when fog was rising from the river that ran below the bluff where the camp was located, we breakfasted and got ready to move out. Our gear was loaded into a four-wheel-drive vehicle; hitched to it was a trailer bearing the canoes in a rack. We got into the high-riding vehicle with the driver and our guides, Willard McCaskill and Cecil Davis. As we lumbered out of the gravel lot at the camp and onto the two-lane macadam road, the driver picked up speed, with the trailer bouncing behind. Through evergreen forest, past a few lonely-looking houses, we sped for possibly a half hour. Then the driver turned our rig into a rough, narrow dirt road along which we clattered for several more miles. I wondered on the way what the driver would do if we met another vehicle on the narrow road. I couldn't imagine backing a trailer loaded with canoes out the curving woods road. Fortunately, we met no one and eventually came to a good-sized clearing beside the river. The stream smelled so fresh! The driver backed the trailer expertly toward the shale river bank, cut the motor, set the brake. The river was clear, gliding smoothly between spruce- and birch-covered banks.

Kenneth had run the river many times previously, so he knew Cecil well, and Willard slightly. They had talked all the way up about the level of the water in the river, about the severity of the previous winter, how many float trips they'd had already this season, the number of salmon taken, and on and on.

"Here we are!" Kenneth said as I slid down out of the vehicle. I could feel his energy, his happiness.

"Ready, love?" he asked, reaching for my hand. "We're going on a trip you'll never forget." And he was right again.

When they unloaded the canoes and slid them down the bank, I noticed the long craft had strips of wood, like runners, attached to the bottom. "It's for reinforcement if we slide over rocks," Cecil told me. Having been in a canoe only on a lake, this news was a bit unsettling, but I kept still. Kenneth had told me there would be times when the float trip turned into a wild ride. We stowed our gear in the craft. In each canoe there was a paddle or two, and a long, wooden pole the guides called a "setting pole," or "set pole." Kenneth boarded the lead canoe with Cecil behind him. They pushed off. I took my place on the seat forward of the guide, and Willard pushed off. We were on the river! Our adventure, finally, had begun.

The river was clear and swift, with trees crowding the banks. Floating quietly along, away from signs and sounds of civilization, was almost hypnotic. I lost track of time and could feel a lightness, a steady relaxation come over me as we slid silently on the water, wondering what was around the next bend. Drifting steadily from pool to pool, we paused to fish at each one that seemed promising. We covered calm water, where the river gurgled over rocks just beneath the surface, but we also rocketed through white water, and took roller coaster dip-and-zoom rides through fast moving current that slapped at midstream boulders. Every inch of it was exhilarating.

Beside some benevolent stretches, the vast evergreen wilderness was splashed with the white of birches. The woodland blanketed rising hills, forming our own universe that we explored by canoe. Bear, moose, and beaver were a few creatures we were told we might see, as well as the beautiful grouse. One day we did come upon a moose standing knee-deep in the river, a great rack crowning its long, mulish head. It was immense, a dark, powerful presence. It jolted the senses. The guides had warned us not to disturb any moose we might encounter, as they can be dangerous when agitated. This one was grazing among lily pads, and we slipped by just as he lifted his great antlered head from the shallows. He didn't retreat. I was breathless, spellbound. He watched us as we passed, then lowered his head once more. It was a moment that still blazes vividly in memory. Seeing an animal in the wild like that is wonderful, and it brings into sharp focus how terrible it would be if a time ever came when there were no wild places, and no wild creatures to see. I pray we will grow wiser and more loving in the care of our world.

The names of the pools and places along the Miramichi spin in memory like the bits of colored glass in a kaleidoscope: Half Moon, Louie Falls, The Sisters, Pork Barrel, Hen and Chicks, Slate Hill, Burnt Hill. But the pieces never stop spinning to form a pattern. The glorious days on the river swirl and eddy cheerfully in remembrance, bringing warmth and a smile. We fished mostly, though not entirely, from the canoes, casting toward a riffle behind a rock where a salmon might rest. Or we'd drift a dry fly down the current toward a dark pool. The angling was intense and tiring to my inexperienced arm and shoulder, but it was great sport. With each inexpert cast, I hoped for a strike, and the miracle of a fish. Kenneth fared far better than I. It was a joy to watch him cast, to overhear his happy talk with Cecil. Kenneth released a number of immature salmon, the shining, quicksilver grilse, but kept one for an evening meal at one of our campsites. I loved hearing the surge of a fish taking the fly, and the whine of the line peeling off the reel as the fish made its run. I loved seeing Kenneth so intensely happy. He took his first fish of the trip on a Bomber. Another, I believe, on a Buck Bug. The legendary, exotic names of the flies are interesting to me, but sometimes incomprehensible.

Running the river was exciting not just for the fishing, but for the downward passage through perilous stretches where huge boulders stood directly in the channel. Other rocks rose like monoliths on each side of the channel. The guide had to have lightning-swift reflexes, strength, the agility of a cat, watchful eyes, and the ability to make quick decisions. My heart pounded one day as we sped toward a mass of granite as big as a refrigerator. We were bearing down on it, and a head-on collision seemed certain. My pulse raced and my eyes widened, when the end of the pole shot past me on the right and thudded into the looming rock. With a quick push, Willard snubbed the canoe to the left of the boulder, and we flew through an opening between two more rocks with inches to spare. The canoe, with Willard steering in the stern, flew through what seemed a mile of foamy rapids, and then lost momentum as the river broadened to a glassy calm.

My guide was a slim, wiry man of medium height. He had penetrating blue eyes and little to say. It was easy to see, however, that he loved the river and loved his work. When the fishing was good, he showed excitement, and even whooped when Kenneth landed a hefty, bright female salmon. He responded politely to my endless questions, and when he saw me writing in my journal, he began to volunteer information about the river, and the flora and fauna. Cecil kidded Willard about this.

"Quietest guide in the camp," Cecil said, cutting a grin in Kenneth's direction, "and now we can't shut him up." I protested that I appreciated Willard's information. Willard took the ribbing good-naturedly, smiling and saying nothing.

We traveled past openings in the woods where ferns were as verdant as in a rain forest. Where sunlight came through the trees, brilliantly colored wildflowers turned the shoreline into an impressionistic painting. Butterflies fluttered among the lavender, yellow, magenta, and white flowers. If our canoe was moving swiftly, and I squinted into the sun, the flowers became a ribbonlike blur of color, like ornamentation on the deep-green wilderness. Having the river and the wilderness to ourselves was lonely in a very touching, romantic way. It was odd how the density of the woods seemed to isolate and magnify each strain of birdsong. To hear a bird sing out clearly and brilliantly when the only sound was that of the canoes moving steadily downstream was as thrilling as a splendid aria. When there is enough silence, we hear things more clearly.

Hooking and bringing to net my first fish on that trip is etched clearly in memory. We were fishing McKeel's Brook. My cast was not a long one. I was aiming for a riffle. The dry fly had barely touched water when there was churning under the fly and the reel sang as line went out. "Got 'im on!" Willard exclaimed, and Kenneth retrieved his line at the other end of the pool. The rod arched, then suddenly the line went slack. "He's turned!" Willard said, his voice tense as the fish turned and ran toward me. I frantically took in line, trying to keep it taut. The salmon was still on the line. The fish made several runs, but I managed to stay calm enough to keep it on and, in a splash of silver, see Willard scoop it up in the landing net.

"Nice bright grilse," Willard shouted to Kenneth and Cecil.

"Good going, Jo!" Kenneth yelled. "What'd you take it on?" I was so excited I could hardly think. "A Woolly-faced McPherson," I said. The three men howled with laughter. In spite of his merriment, Willard looked questioningly at me. It all happened so quickly.

"Release it," I said, quietly. They told me later that the correct name of the fly was Rat-faced McDougall. "I knew it was some kind of odd Scotsman!" I retorted. The thrill of that success is as bright today as it was all those years ago.

We spent one night in a tiny cabin, the components of which had been brought to the site by canoe. There were cots, a couple of chairs, a lantern. And best of all, a gravity-fed shower with icy water. After time on the river with only quick washes at the river's edge, that shower was a luxury, even if it was bone chilling. It was there, too, I believe, that Kenneth and Cecil walked into the forest, Kenneth toting a light rod for trout. Willard busied himself with camp chores while I did a bit of hand laundry. After a while, the two returned, muttering about the mosquitoes and blackflies at the trout stream, but proudly bringing a mess of "brookies" for supper.

The guides were surprisingly capable campfire cooks. They made a kind of flat, hoecake-style bread, warmed tinned vegetables, baked potatoes in the ashes, and prepared cured meat and, of course, fish. Fried in bacon fat until crisp on the outside, the small brook trout were delicate and delicious, with firm pink flesh. Brook trout, baked beans, and very, very strong hot tea, served by the river, seemed a feast for royalty.

I shall never forget the sunny days and chilly nights on that float trip, nor the excitement of running Burnt Hill rapids, with water splashing over the bow and frothing at the gunwales. It was like riding a runaway horse. It was so exciting I couldn't resist shouting "Whoooo-eee!" as the canoe dipped and ran, with Willard keeping the bucking craft in the channel. When we shot out of the rapids, it was both a relief and a disappointment. The quiet times were even more impressive: casting, gliding downstream, looking down into the clear water. In different stretches, I saw shale, rocks, and slate on the river bottom. When we were traversing rapids or dodging boulders, I gave no thought to what was below us. What I did consider at such times was the possibility of the guide being lifted out of the canoe by the long pole, if it should jam among the rocks. This could happen easily if the guide didn't quickly realize the pole was stuck, and turn it loose before the canoe moved on without him. Fortunately, this did not happen. But we saw a setting pole sticking up out of the river like a channel marker at one rocky stretch. No doubt a guide had lost it.

When I probe my memory about that wonderful trip, the one element that always surfaces is the feeling of joy. Sunlight dappling the river. The swish of fly line. The smell of the campfire. Counting the stars that canopied our campsites. Sharing something so special with someone you love. And the bittersweet final stretch of river, before putting in on the sand at Push and Be Damned. And happiness. Abiding happiness.

Before we went home, the guides tied a fly in my honor: The Woolly-faced McPherson. It is a wicked-looking bit of clipped deer hair with exaggerated wings. We may have been among the last to float the river , because it no longer was an option offered by most outfitters. That was the first time I took the float trip down the Main Southwest Miramichi, and the last time Kenneth ran the river.

Miramichi Epilogue

We went salmon fishing in New Brunswick many times after that, staying at Campbell's fish camp and at a cabin overlooking the river at Upper Blackville. Kenneth loved wading the river and this provided him that opportunity. When I became visually impaired, I gave up fly-fishing, and contented myself with enjoying nature, and watching Kenneth cast what a guide said to me was a "foine line." These trips provided some memorable moments, too. Like Kenneth slogging up the riverbank in his waders, holding up a fine Atlantic salmon for me to see. And there was the time, at Campbell's camp, when the smokehouse (in which salmon were being smoked) beside a small pond caught fire.

It happened while the guests at the camp were assembled on the deck, having drinks before dinner. Kenneth was wearing a pair of bright-red corduroy trousers and a plaid shirt. Another male guest, who was about Kenneth's size, was kidding my husband about his bright britches, and suggested that Kenneth should will them to him, since he felt sure they would fit him, too. It was at that point that someone yelled "Fire!" and the men ran down to the smokehouse to try to put out the fire. In the melee, the man who had been kidding Kenneth managed to set his own pant's leg on fire, and had to step into the pond to put it out. He also managed to rip his pants. The smokehouse was a lost cause, and the only thing to do was move back and watch it burn, which we did. It was a smoldering ruin when the fire truck finally got there.

We regrouped on the deck. Towels were handed 'round so the men could wipe smudgy faces and hands. Everyone was talking at once. Kenneth was smudged, but his clothing was intact. Not so the fellow who had been ribbing Kenneth about his red britches—that man's pants were torn, seared, muddy. Kenneth took one look, walked over, quickly unzipped his red pants, stepped out of them, and handed them to the man in the ragged trousers.

"You wanted them, here they are," Kenneth said, handing the bright-red pants to the other guest. A howl of laughter went up among the fisherfolk. In plaid shirt, tattersall boxers, socks, and deck shoes, Kenneth went off down the path to our cabin, with me in tow, to change for dinner. In spite of the fact that the smokehouse had burned down, the mood at dinner that night was very lighthearted. The man who had been kidding Kenneth was wearing the bright-red corduroy trousers.

I remember another time when Kenneth was fishing from one side of what is called "The Home Pool." On the other side, casting a very long line, was Ted Williams, the baseball legend. We had met before. Kenneth was an avid dry fly fisherman. Ted Williams preferred the wet fly. So, at dusk, when neither fisherman had met with success, Ted Williams and a friend of his invited us to join them for a sundowner. I am six feet tall, but when I stood beside Ted Williams, I felt petite. He is, as everyone knows, a tall, handsome, well-built man. And he has great presence. Anyway, the four of us trooped into the trailer owned by Ted Williams's friend. Libations were poured and we exchanged ideas on the best ways to cook certain game. And fish. Then the conversation turned, inevitably, to the matter of dry fly-fishing versus wet fly-fishing. The proponents of each took sides, and the discussion was polite, but heated. The men kindled the conversation with another drink. There was no winner. But it was Ted Williams's birthday, and unless the debate ended, he would be late for his birthday party. To demonstrate his dexterity and, I imagine, to end the discussion dramatically, Ted Williams suddenly stood on his hands in the cramped living room of the fisherman's getaway. Standing on his hands, his long legs close to the ceiling, he laughed, and flipped back over as the place shuddered. Hearty goodbyes were said all 'round. But the debate hung in the air, to be argued by fishermen for years to come. And the river was still there, for tomorrow.

On the Loose in Heath and Heather

The spare beauty of the Highlands was tranquilizing as we sped past mile after mile of heather-covered moorland. The moors were in October dress. A bluish haze seemed to hold just over the reddish-brown heather, which stretched toward a pale amber horizon that met a soft gray sky. "Less truly is more," I thought. It was splendid. Kenneth was driving the little English Ford at a snappy clip on a nearly empty road that curled steadily upward through the rolling moors. We had hardly seen another car in the last twenty miles. I was in that near somnolent state of one who is totally relaxed and absorbed in the scenery when we rounded a curve and Kenneth stood on the brakes and yelped, "*Geeeezus!*" I pitched forward and caught myself as the tires squealed and the car slid to a sideways halt.

"Baaaa! Baaaa!" came from every side of us. We were surrounded by a flock of very calm sheep. My heart pounded from their sudden appearance on the road. It was a big flock. Kenneth looked at me, shaking his head in a gesture of relief. It felt as if we were in an echo chamber as the woolly animals went past, bleating to one another.

"Guess I'd better slow down," Kenneth said. I nodded, "Yes." When the flock finally had crossed the road, Kenneth started the car, and we drove off at a slower pace.

We had spent the last two weeks jaunting around Scotland, staying at inns and stately homes open to travelers, and playing golf. We stayed at St. Andrews and played the old course at the Royal and Ancient Club. Even in October, there was a brisk wind on the links, and I had to break out a windbreaker to cover my thick sweater on the first tee. The two caddies had worn what looked like abbreviated tweed overcoats and wool scarves. On some windy holes, the scarves flapped downwind à la the Red Baron. We were both hitting the ball fairly well, but in the stiff wind, our shots often fell short. I hit my ball into a neck-deep trap that was cuffed on the front side with what looked like a hedge of sugarcane. It was gorse. I descended the ladder, as had legions of golfers before me, and my feet sank into sand. I looked forward. The gorse curved over the trap like one of those huge waves you see in Japanese woodblock prints. *Awesome* would be the correct word. I thrashed around in there with an assortment of irons, finally climbed out red-faced and frustrated. And then we went on to find other traps, several burns—and rarely the hole in par. But Kenneth and I both cleared the burn on the eighteenth fairway and putted out like proper golfers on the last green.

We played the course the next day with more success. Perhaps the gods had mercy. We went on to Gleneagles, Turnberry, and others, and no matter how our golf games went, we had a fine time. It seemed to me that there were just about as many (or more) distillers of Scotch whiskey as there were golf courses, because Kenneth dragged me on side trips to visit the distilleries. There was much talk of color, "peatiness," purity. After several of these sojourns, Kenneth reminded me that I had dragged *him* all through the Loire Valley and the great vineyards and châteaus only two years ago. "Besides," he said (rather sanctimoniously, I thought), "am I not taking you all the way up to the Pentland Firth to check out your roots?" He was indeed.

"That's true. But remember I went with you to your great-grandfather's village in Wales. Remember that place we couldn't pronounce?" I countered.

We were, in fact, on the last leg of our vacation. Like all Americans with Scottish forebears, I wanted to see where my father's people had come from. So we were driving through the moors on our way to Thurso, on the northeast tip of Scotland.

"And may I remind you that you are also going to get together with another publisher up there in that area? So agreeing to go that far north was not entirely magnanimous."

"It'll be fun," he replied. "We'll be there before dark. I'll meet with Reggie for lunch tomorrow so we can, I hope, conclude that agreement on our joint publishing venture. Maybe. But I expect Reg will squeeze one more trip to New York out of the deal before it's over with." I laughed. The negotiations between the publishing house of which my husband was president and the European firm that Reginald directed had gone on amiably, but interminably.

The publisher, whom I shall call Reginald Ferguson, had come to New York a number of times to discuss what Kenneth called the "minutia" of the joint venture. One evening when Reggie came to dinner at our apartment, he brought a brace of red grouse—which he had smuggled through customs by the simple ploy of putting the birds (still "en plumage") under his hat. He demonstrated the trick over cocktails before dinner. Reggie is tall, dark haired, and dark eyed.

His face crinkles easily into a smile. He is a man who likes to laugh, whose manner is easy and genteel. (His wife, Daphne, is fair haired, pretty, and very much the aristocrat, also.) During Reggie's visit to New York, he and Kenneth had agreed to get together in Scotland in October and discuss their joint venture. And Reggie said that we must visit their country place in Scotland while we were abroad.

And here we were, heading for Pentland Firth, and Thurso, which is situated on Thurso Bay. The last few miles seemed to drag by, but soon we were cruising down the main street of Thurso. It is a small town, the street lined with typical village shops. The inn/hotel was in the middle of town, its weathered facade even with the village shops.

"There's the inn," I said, thinking Kenneth had overlooked it. "I saw it," Kenneth said, "but let's take a little tour of the town before we check in."

"Great," I nodded.

The tour didn't take long. We drove straight ahead, to a little square, in the center of which was a tall statue of a man. Kenneth pulled over so we could read the inscription at the foot of the monument.

"Well, I'll be darned," he laughed, "take a look at that." I was as surprised as he was. The monument was a statue of Sir John Sinclair, "father of agriculture in Scotland." Or words to that effect. Memory does pale, unfortunately.

"Well! I certainly hope he is one of my ancestors. Maybe it would explain why there have been so many generations of farmers in our family. Think love of the soil is a genetic thing?" I asked. We drove around the square, turned down a parallel street that overlooked the water, and there, on display, was the original town pump. We drove on, turned again, and soon parked in front of the hotel. We toted our own baggage inside, where we were greeted cordially, and went to our room, which overlooked the main street. The room was spotlessly clean, furnished with the essentials. It was pleasant, but with no frills and foolery. Kenneth sat on the bed, testing it.

"Flinty folks, these Highlanders," he grinned, getting very little feedback from the firm mattress. Perhaps it was because I was tired, or perhaps it was not memorable, but I have absolutely no recall of where or on what we dined. I do remember scones and jam and strong, hot tea the next morning. We slept late (possibly scandalizing the early-rising proprietors), so by the time we had breakfasted, it was almost time for Kenneth to meet Reggie. They would talk business over lunch. Reggie was right on time. He looked around the small lobby with interest while we exchanged greetings. It was clear he'd never set foot in the hotel. "And how will you be occupying your time, Jo?" Reggie inquired.

"I will look around in the shops. And I spotted a very nice antiques store that I want to visit. I'll have a fine time, don't you worry."

As soon as they left, I got into the little car and took another spin through town. I drove around the area a bit, prowled in shops, saving for last the antiques shop that looked so intriguing. I noticed a discreet inscription on the window indicating that Her Majesty the Queen might buy from this establishment. I opened the door and stepped into the spacious shop. Faint traces of beeswax and lemon oil lingered in the air. Or was it potpourri? There was a corridor of light near the front windows. The rest of the interior, with chests, tables, cupboards, chairs, and a conglomeration of other antiques, was in half-light and deep shadow. I sniffed again. Perhaps that pleasant overtone of well-cherished furniture was lavender. Hard to tell but it was oddly stirring. It seemed there was no one in the shop. I moved among the polished tables and chests, admiring fine porcelains and silver candelabra, making as much noise as I could without sounding like the proverbial bull in a china shop. No one appeared. Finally, I called out. "Helloo. Anybody home?" A door swished, and I heard someone say in an odd voice, "Good afternoon." I looked around, but could see no one.

"Hello?" I repeated, confused. Again the small voice, sounding almost as if from a distance, said "Good afternoon." It was a tiny voice, with Scottish accent. I looked around. "Fine afternoon," the voice repeated. Where had I heard that voice? Yes—as a child, when a tiny man in a bellhop's uniform sang out in a television ad, "Call for Phillip Mor-ris!" That was it. A midget advertising cigarettes. Just as I remembered this, the tiny voice was close to me, sounding as though it came from my feet. I looked down into the smiling face of a red-haired midget wearing a finely tailored, miniature suit. I restrained my surprise. The petite proprietor spoke again in his fine Scottish accent. "I apologize. I did not realize you were in the shop." He looked me over, staring up at me. My six-foot height must have seemed like the Matterhorn to the polite little man. "From the United States, are you? I noticed your auto drive into town yesterday evening."

"Yes," I said, stammering a little. "Yes, we are. Yes. From New York."

"Oooh," he replied, the single word full of knowledge and perhaps a hint of disdain.

"But I'm from North Carolina. The South." I went on, feeling foolish. His eyebrows, like two tiny red woolly worms, shot up in amazement. "Do look 'round," he said cordially, thoroughly aware that his appearance had startled me, and amused by my discomfiture. He had been through this before.

"Are you looking for anything in particular?" He was polite, self-assured, willing to be of service. I imagined that he could have sold the queen anything without the least bit of trouble. Not even the queen could ruffle that politely controlled demeanor.

"No," I said lamely. "Just looking."

"Please look as long as you wish," he said. "If I may be of assistance, just ask. We do, by the way, ship our antiques anywhere in the world."

"Thank you," I said, staring at his tiny, tiny, highly polished black shoes. He disappeared. Literally vanished into the shadows. I wondered if he darted under a table. I soon forgot the midget anti-quarian as I browsed among the fine collection of furniture. I pictured in my mind at least a dozen pieces that would look wonderful in our New York apartment. The price tags were also tiny, as if in keeping with the size of the shop owner. The figures were written in a fine, delicate hand. Nevertheless, the sums were not of midget pro-portion. I wistfully admired the highboys, corner chairs, and side-boards. Then my eyes fell on a delicate pembroke table, Queen Anne period, with cabriole legs, and a finely turned stretcher between them. The table had a lustrous patina, two drop leaves, a single drawer. I looked at the price tag and walked away. I wandered around the room some more, but kept returning to the pembroke table. As I stared at it wistfully, the tiny voice floated toward me.

"That's a fine table, made in the Orkneys around 1740."

"Yes," I agreed. "It's lovely. I like it very much." He came toward me, noticing my hesitation.

"Perhaps you'd like your husband to have a look at it, if you're interested in it. Remember, we ship anywhere in the world. It is no problem."

"I would like Kenneth to see it, if he gets back before your shop closes."

He assured me they were open late and in the course of our conversation I told him that we came to Thurso so that I could see where my ancestors came from.

"You're a Sinclair, are you?" he asked. "Then you'll want to ride out on the moor to see the Sinclair hunting lodge. Unfortunately, the head of your clan is away, but you can see the place, at least." I was disappointed, because I had intended to telephone and say hello. I am sure that Scots are regularly besieged with American tourists in search of their roots. Nevertheless, no matter how tacky, that was my plan as well. I thanked him and said I'd better be going.

"If you have time," he said, "you might want to go around to my sister's shop. She has less furniture and more porcelain, silver, and decorative items. Paintings, things like that."

"How do I get there?" I asked, wondering if she might be a midget, too.

"Go to the end of the street, turn left, drive along the water, and you'll see the sign for her shop."

I thanked him and left, thinking about Kenneth's reaction to the pembroke table. And the price.

I followed his directions and sure enough, there was another antiques shop. I parked the car and got out. The brother midget must have called the sister midget before I arrived, because no sooner had I crossed the gloomy threshold than a tiny voice called out, "Welcome. Come in." I went into a fascinating, haphazardly arranged world of other people's treasures from the past. Portraits dour and merry stared into time. Bronzes, porcelains, copper, brass were everywhere. There were endless pairs of brass candlesticks. Some flatware, copper kettles, andirons, linens, unrecognizable objects, a top hat, a china umbrella stand bristling with canes, and fringed umbrellas. The diminutive lady had curly red hair, a merry face. She had on a plaid skirt that must have come from the children's section of some store, and a matched set of wee sweaters that looked hand knitted. She skipped along in front of me, pulling on overhead lights by means of a series of strings that looked like rigging in a ship. I wondered who had rigged it for her. She stepped up on a stool, and reaching above her, switched on a lamp that seemed as tall as she. A pool of light fell on a collection of Battersea boxes, silver thimbles, bits of jewelry. I had a wonderful time plundering in the shop and talking with the warm and witty little lady. I bought a few odds and ends and took my leave, thanking her for her courtesy.

I was resting with my feet up on the foot of the bed when Kenneth returned.

"Hi, love," I greeted him. "How'd it go with Reggie?" He sat in a narrow, upholstered chair. "This chair smells a little musty," he said. "No heat," I replied. "But plenty of wool blankets. Even if it's cold tonight, we'll be warm." He looked around the room hopefully, looking for heat outlets. "There's an electric heater," he said with relief, pointing at an ancient, small heater enclosed in a wire grid. It was far too small to do any good in the room, but I kept still.

"Tell me about your lunch with Reggie," I said.

Not to be put off from his preoccupation with the weather, he said, "You do remember we drove through a snow flurry on the way up here? Just before we encountered the sheep?" I certainly did re-member. It had been stunning. The sun was out, the day was clear, when suddenly we encountered a shadow on the road, and the next thing we knew we were engulfed in a thick flurry of snow. We drove out of it almost before we had time to realize that we were in a mini-snowstorm.

"You think it might snow?" he asked, going to the window and staring suspiciously at the sky.

"No! That was just a freaky little bit of snow. Now tell me about your meeting." He sat back down and reached for a bottle of Scotch on a table near the chair. He stood up and walked to the old-fashioned bathroom sink.

"It went fine. We actually signed the contract. But Reggie may come to New York just to talk over a few details." He grinned. "I'm celebrat-ing. Join me?"

"Not right now," I said. "Have your drink and then there's something I want you to see." He looked at me over his lowered spectacles. "Something at the antiques shop, by any chance?" he queried, taking a sip of his drink. "Maybe I'd better brace up with a *couple* of drinks."

"Yes, at the antiques shop. And no, you don't need the second drink. But you might have to brace yourself a bit. But just keep in mind that anything we might buy here will cost far more in New York."

"Oh, Lord," he moaned. "I'd better hide my wallet." Seeing my disappointed look, he added, "We'll go look as soon as I've finished my drink."

I waited patiently while he slowly sipped his Scotch and water. I did not tell him that the proprietor was a midget. I wickedly wanted to see how Kenneth handled the situation. I felt I had handled it badly.

Kenneth and I entered the antiques shop. Immediately, the child-like, cordial voice of the proprietor greeted us. "Hello again, Mrs. Northrop. Good afternoon, Mr. Northrop. I see your wife persuaded you to come have a look at the table."

For a moment, but only for a moment, Kenneth looked confused. But as the well-tailored midget approached, Kenneth looked down, extended his hand, and said, "Afternoon." He shot an I'll-get-even-with-you glance at me and said, "Wonderful shop you have here." I made hurried introductions. I imagined my voice was unusually high pitched and squeaky.

"What is it that Jo thinks I should see?" Kenneth asked.

The dapper shopkeeper darted ahead, the top of his head not far above low tables, and far below buffets, desks, and chests. Kenneth looked at the table we indicated. He snatched the drawer out, tapped the bottom. He rubbed his hand over the lustrous tabletop.

"Nice," he said to me. We were high above the little gentleman, so we could speak softly without fear of being heard. Kenneth murmured to me, "How much?"

I pointed to the unobtrusive price tag. Kenneth turned it over, stared, then dropped it as if it had burned his fingers. The shopkeeper, accustomed to just such reactions (from almost everyone but the queen, I imagined), said in his most fluid little voice, "It's an exceptional piece. Early. In perfect condition. And we ship anywhere in the world." Like a man hoping for a reprieve, Kenneth asked, "Do you really want this table? It seems awfully small for a big amount of money."

He and the proprietor laughed together, bass and soprano mingling mirthfully at the feeble joke.

"I want it only if you do, Kenneth. By New York standards, it's a very good buy. It would be a splendid remembrance of our trip to Scotland."

Giving in gracefully, Kenneth gave it one last shot. "I don't want to use our traveler's checks for this purchase," he said, looking hopefully at the proprietor. I knew he was hoping that would queer the transaction, save him a fair sum of money. Had his move worked, I couldn't have blamed him, and he'd only have had to bid a regretful antiques shopkeeper farewell. But the little man said, "That is no problem at all, Mr. Northrop. We wouldn't want you to find yourself running low on funds while on your trip. We'll be happy to take your personal check." Checkmate. Kenneth signed the receipt and wrote the check. I smiled broadly at both men. Kenneth bent down to offer his hand to the smiling midget. They shook hands. Kenneth looked

at him and said, "A fellow can get into a lot of trouble in Thurso."
They both laughed. When we left the shop, the little man was still
laughing his high, crackling laugh.

"Bloody little bandit!" Kenneth huffed. "You should pardon the
pun, but pound for pound, he gave a drubbing." Kenneth smiled.

"It's a wonderful table. It'll look great in our apartment." I
changed the subject. "Are we invited to the Fergusons' for dinner?
Reggie mentioned it briefly before you went off this noon."

"Yes," Kenneth said. "Drinks at seven, dinner at eight. Reggie
said it's about a forty-five minute drive to their country place."

"Do you know how to get there?" I asked. "Did Reggie give you
directions?"

"South," Kenneth said, "Ferguson House. He said all the local
folk know where it is."

We were both looking forward to the evening. Dressed in best
bib and tucker, we got into the little Ford and headed south. And
south and south and south.

"Do you think we may have gone too far south?" I asked, glanc-
ing at my watch. We had been on the road fifty minutes.

"I'm looking for the turn," Kenneth said. "It's Bannock Burn,
or something like that."

My heart sank. My dear husband had listened to the directions
very casually, always certain that he could find his way.

"Kenneth, do you mean to say that you don't know the exact
name of the road?"

"This must be it," he retorted, turning sharply right into a narrow country lane. We drove by burns, berms, hummocks, and a sea of

heather. It was getting later. I was exasperated. Kenneth was cross because it was clear he didn't know which way to go.

"I can't believe that two men who head large companies can't get their directions straight," I muttered. I was tired of making right turns, left turns, U turns.

Kenneth tightened his grip on the steering wheel and doggedly drove on. Finally, relaxing a bit, he said, "We'll ask for directions if we ever see a human being. So far, I've seen nothing but sheep."

We drove on, round a hill, down a vale. Finally we came to a crossroad. A man was in the yard in front of a small house. Kenneth stopped the car, got out, and approached him. They talked, and the man pointed left, waving and gesturing. Kenneth was paying close attention. He came back to the car and flopped in the driver's seat. "Hell," he said, "he never heard of Ferguson House. Didn't know any Fergusons lived around here. He said we might turn left here, in front of his house, and go into the small village up the road and ask if anyone around there has ever heard of Ferguson House."

"Let's just go back to the hotel," I said. "It's so late. We can telephone them and explain what happened. They can blame it on Ugly Americans."

"I would if I could," Kenneth laughed, "but I'll be damned if I know how to find Thurso. I admit I'm lost."

The situation was so hopelessly ludicrous, we both began to laugh. We sat in the car, laughing and laughing. The man, standing in his yard, watched us solemnly. He turned his back to us, and shaking his head, walked toward his front door. Kenneth started the car and turned left on the road in front of the little house. Hearing the car, the man turned around and watched. As we passed, I waved and the man, a look of puzzlement on his face, waved back.

It seemed like twenty miles of twisting and turning on the narrow country road before we saw the lights of the village. Darkness had fallen quickly, like a sodden black blanket. I didn't think I'd ever seen a countryside so dark. In the village, Kenneth spotted a battered taxi and got out to ask directions from the driver. There was a lot of conversation, and I saw Kenneth hand the driver some money. Kenneth hurried back to the car.

"Pay dirt!" he shouted. "The driver actually knows where Ferguson House is, and will lead us to it. He said we might get lost on these back roads. I hope that car of his will make it." This struck us both funny, and we howled with laughter. The taxi set off at a fast pace, and Kenneth fell in behind him.

"Wait a minute, Kenneth," I implored. "It's after nine o'clock already. We can't go barging in at their house over two hours late."

"We have to," Kenneth said, deadpan. "I have to get directions from Reggie for the way back to the hotel."

The situation was so foolish, there seemed to be nothing to do but continue on to our host and hostess's. I hoped they would be good humored about it. I needn't have worried.

We had driven for another interminable twenty minutes, winding and weaving through the dark countryside, when the taxi stopped at a narrow drive. The driver turned his left turn signal on and tooted his horn. Kenneth whirled into the drive and the taxi roared off.

We drove along the narrow lane beside a hedgerow. We passed what appeared to be a stable, drove past a horse van, and parked in front of the immense country house. I could hear dogs barking. Kenneth took my hand and we moved in the dark toward the house. Suddenly a light came on, and the front door was flung open. "Come in!" Reggie said, waving us inside. "It's senseless to ask if you were lost. Or perhaps it is the reputation of our cooking that has made you late?"

By this time, Daphne, who seemed a bit starry eyed, the two children, three or four Labrador retrievers, and a clutch of small, hairy dogs were all around us. The Labs woofed, the little dogs yapped. The children were polite, and Kenneth, Reggie, Daphne, and I were all talking at once. We trooped into a cozy study, where a fire was burning. The dogs finished their sniffing inspection of the newcomers and the children disappeared. The little dogs dispersed. (Corgis? Scotties? Westies? In the frenzy, there was no time to determine their breeds.)

We settled in comfortable chairs around the fire, and I had a chance to apologize quietly to our hostess. I told her that I knew it was shameless to appear almost three hours after the appointed time, but that we really hadn't a clue as to the way back to the hotel.

"Do not worry," she said. "What are three hours in a lifetime?" It was then I realized what her starry-eyed gaze and slightly blurred speech meant. She had taken the precaution of bracing herself for the possibility that we Americans might actually arrive three hours late for dinner. When Reggie passed drinks around, I noticed that it was martinis that had brought her to this benevolent, forgiving, and philosophical state.

"Three hours are as nothing in a lifetime," I agreed, sipping my drink. Daphne and I carried on a rather surreal conversation while

Reggie and Kenneth talked shotguns, gunning dogs, and grouse shooting. Before long, it was apparent that we were, in spite of the hour,
having dinner. The children were serving. No doubt the help had
long since gone. We went into the dining room, which was dimly lit
with a scattering of candles. It was also chilly. We were seated around
a table that sprawled into the gloom. We chatted as Reggie poured
wine. The children came round with salvers and bowls filled with
unidentifiable food. We each took a small slice of what must have
been meat. When their son had gone round with the meat, he placed
the tray back on the sideboard and covered it with a domed silver lid.
It seemed redundant, somehow. Then we were served anonymous vegetables and a sauce for the meat. The meat was cold, the vegetables
were cold, the sauce was cold. There was nothing to do but talk ani-
matedly in order to camouflage one's dispirited attempt to eat the
three-hours-cold meal. The dining room was positively abuzz with
conversation. The children took our nearly full plates away, and
brought a limp, warm salad. We all talked madly while stirring the
withered greens around. Then came a warm dessert that I suspect
should have been cold. Something had puddled in the manner of
melted ice cream. We all stirred that around vigorously, talking and
quaffing Reggie's excellent wine. When the meal was blessedly over,
we retired to the study. Reggie brought out brandy. Daphne was nearly
prone on a sofa, and was gently singing to herself. When Kenneth
refused brandy, I knew he was determined to find our way back to the
hotel as quickly as possible. Reggie's good will and intelligent conversation never wavered. I was light-headed from drinking wine without food. Kenneth was fine, and I was about to give him a signal that

we should leave when I caught his eye, and he was giving me the same sign.

Kenneth listened very carefully to Reggie's directions. So did I. I had never felt more tired in my life as we bid our goodbyes. Reggie and the pack of dogs saw us out (very gratefully, I expect). I apologized again for our tardiness, and Reggie brushed my apology aside. "I'll go in now and have a brandy. Sorry you won't join me." Gentlemanly to the bitter end. From the study, Daphne sang out, "Bye, bye birdies. Sorry to see you go." We hurried to the car as Reggie stood among his dogs waving as we drove off.

I was quiet. Spent. At the end of the lane, Kenneth said, "It's probably a good thing we signed the contract at lunch!"

We made it to the hotel without a single wrong turn. I suppressed the urge to say, "Why couldn't you do that on the way over." We crawled under the heavy covers in the chilly bedroom and slept soundly until morning.

Over scones and tea, Kenneth said, "OK, girl, this is your last chance to track down the Sinclairs."

"The head of the clan is away," I said, "but I'd like to see Sinclair's Bay, and go out on the moor to see the hunting lodge."

"I hope it's not as hard to find as Ferguson House," Kenneth laughed.

It wasn't, but the drive across the moor to the lodge was long and straight. Finally, we came to it. "Very impressive," I said. "I wonder if there is a portrait in there of a Margaret Joan Sinclair of another time."

"Not a chance," Kenneth shot back. "There's only one of your kind!"

"Should I say thank you?"

"I take the Fifth," Kenny grinned, turning the car back along the rutted road in the direction from which we had come. We bumped along through the hazy heather. Kenneth stopped at one point to watch some men who had been "stagging." As I understood it, the hunters concealed themselves in the heather at a location where they could spot a stag. I am not certain if they crept toward the stag or not, but when a stag was within range, they'd fire. The hunters we saw had been successful. They had a huge red deer on a sledge pulled by stout ponies. When a stag was downed, the hunters would fetch the ponies and sledge, load the stag on the sledge, and drag it off the moor. Kenneth was fascinated by the process, and enjoyed talking to the men. As we drove toward town, I tried to imagine my ancestors walking on those moors. Kenneth was right. Flinty folk.

We checked out of the hotel and headed south for a final round of golf and then the flight home. As we drove past the antiques shop, the red-haired midget proprietor was standing in the door. He gave us a brief, tiny wave.

As we drove away from Thurso and retraced our route through the bleakly beautiful moors, an odd, bittersweet feeling welled up in me, as if I might miss the Highlands.

Shotgun: Part of Pa's Fishing Tackle

My family discovered it was not entirely due to the danger of cottonmouth moccasins that my father took a shotgun when he went fishing at a nearby creek. There are plenty of snakes on the mossy banks and in the murky waters of the upper Lumber River in North Carolina, where my father often went fishing. (To most Tarheels, the upper Lumber River is known by the chilling name of Drowning Creek.) It is black, fast, and treacherous water that looks like iced tea where it fans out over sand bars. It is soberingly cold, as many a careless boater has discovered. It is also mysteriously beautiful, and my father enjoyed fishing it. Sometimes he went with a friend, but more often, with my brother-in-law, Ned, who is a skillful fisherman and handler of a Carolina creek boat.

Now and again my father would go alone, just fish along the bank, casting a Jitterbug or Lucky 13 toward the middle of the creek, and into eddies. Casting from either side of Drowning Creek was not always easy, for there was thick brush along the banks, and at many of the best pools, limbs of great water oaks reached far out over the water. This presented a considerable problem for my father, who loved fishing, but admittedly was no Izaak Walton.

Pa was an avid sportsman all of his life. He loved the outdoors in a way that was definitely contagious. He had fine reflexes for gunning, and enjoyed a reputation among his friends as "a good shot." He did a lot of hunting in his day, and like most outdoorsmen, loved talking about it. (And I always loved listening to the talk, especially when Pa and his friend "Turkey" Lacey McFadyen swapped stories.) Pa willingly, if not always tolerantly, taught any of his children and grandchildren who expressed an interest, how to shoot and handle a gun safely. He expected excellence from his kinfolk, so he was not always a study in patience. He knew what he was doing and he wanted to be sure we knew, too.

My father had a natural sense of reserve and dignity typical of a true countryman, balanced with a wry sense of humor. But I believe he may also have had a streak of the test pilot or stock car driver in him. When he went afield, literally, in one of his endless string of Ford station wagons, his raciest Scottish genes came into play. He drove those wagons across cotton and cornfields, through scrub brush and blackjack saplings. Spotting a deep ditch between him and a thicket that might harbor a covey of quail, he'd floor the accelerator and "let 'er rip."

My father looked on hunting as pure adventure, and every outing in his wagon was a steeplechase. Any motor company would have done well to let Pa test the indestructibility of its station wagons. He said a station wagon wasn't worth a damn until it had dog tracks and bird feathers inside, and dents and brush scratches outside.

My mother often complained that when she rode to church in his wagons, she was likely to discover quail feathers sticking to her Sunday clothes. "I looked like I was molting," she'd laugh. My father usually retorted that quail feathers on a dress were no less civilized than fancy feathers on a hat. We attended the Presbyterian church of which Pa's great-grandfather was founder. But quite reasonably, Pa was not fond of long sermons. If a sermon wandered on, Pa would studiedly examine the hour on his watch and then wind it. Loudly. He was giving notice that the sermon was keeping him from giving his pointers a run before Sunday dinner. More often as not, the minister was coming to our house to share that dinner.

As fine a shot as my father was, he was hopeless at repairing anything. He cheerfully admitted this, and sensibly left such things to people with smaller hands, greater patience, and greater aptitude. Pa was interested in what made things tick, but not in keeping them ticking. He said he couldn't build a hog trough that wouldn't leak. Once, though, he decided to nail down a squeaky stair that annoyed him. In doing so, he dropped the hammer, which bounced down the stairs and through a large window on the stair landing. He ruefully called both a carpenter and a glazier.

Just as my father was amused by his own ineptitude at repairing things, he happily admitted that he was not a classic fisherman. A fly rod's need for delicate handling was beyond him. He loved his spinning reel and the places it took him. He preferred freshwater fishing, and went at it joyfully and noisily—on lake, farm pond, creek, and river. He clattered reel and oars in a boat, thumped the ashes from his pipe on the gunwales, whistled tunelessly and cheerfully while he frequently changed plugs. The consensus among his family and anyone who fished with him was that he could make more racket with a tackle box than any man who ever fished.

We often remarked at the deplorable condition of his lures, wondering at their scars, their lack of paint, their pitted bodies. Then my brother-in-law got the truth. One day, Ned and my father were casting for bass on the calm surface of a well-stocked farm pond. Standing on the grassy bank, they watched in amazement the irregular, dipping and bobbing motion of the plug my father was reeling in. "Tom," Ned said to Pa, "something's wrong with that plug. Did you hook some lilypads?"

My father continued reeling the wildly bobbing plug. When it cleared the water, Ned laid down his fly rod and went over to have a look. Dangling at the end of Pa's line, listing heavily to one side, was a battered and ancient-looking plug. "Maybe it's too old," Ned suggested.

"No," Pa replied. "It's new. I just broke it in last week over on Drowning Creek."

"Well, what in the world happened to it?" Ned asked in astonishment.

"I had to shoot it out of some water-oak limbs over the creek," Pa admitted sheepishly. "I hated to lose a brand new plug."

Ned roared with laughter. "Tom, it's so full of birdshot I'm surprised it even floats!"

"Well, I guess I'll just have to save it for swift water," said Pa, tossing the plug into his tackle box. Noisily.

That's the way it was with my father. He was good at direct and sometimes unorthodox solutions to life's problems. He was a sport, and after all these years, I still miss him. I hope heaven has good fishing waters and many wild coveys.

A Sense of Place

Fall came subtly, in quick bursts of cool air, and in the crunch of drying grass underfoot. River water and creek water both lost some of their murkiness when cooler weather came. The fields would be thick with milkweed, drying grasses, faded Queen Anne's lace, and rattly seed pods. Combines in the fields, harvesting soybeans and corn, created miniature dust storms behind them. Pumpkins and colorful squashes and red and yellow corn were in the roadside stands, and the spicy scent of chrysanthemum filled rooms where the flowers stood in shaggy jewel-toned bouquets. When only bean and corn stubble was left in the field, the landscape, almost imperceptibly, faded to amber, then tones of beige and brown—like a monochromatic painting. The river glinted blue in the autumn light.

A Barn Holds to the Land

Faded an earthy sienna that only time and weather can achieve, the old barn sagged gently toward the creek. Like an experienced seaman who adjusts his steps to the motion of the sea, the barn, almost with a kind of structural wisdom, held firmly, beautifully to the land.

The men who raised that stoutly pegged and beamed structure knew what they were doing. They also knew something about the bitterly cold winters in those New York State foothills—the barn was only a short distance from the back door of our stone farmhouse. It was evident from its construction that it was a barn built for a working farm. After nearly two centuries, it showed no signs of critical decay. Bright paint and new siding would have been as out of place on that elderly building as bright makeup would be on an aristocratic, gray-haired lady. The natural beauty, the "bones" of the barn, like the natural beauty of the lady who has borne up well with the passage of time, needed no enhancement. It was shaded by apple and maple trees, and in front, a hawthorn tree that in spring was thick with magenta blossoms.

I often sat on the screened porch at the back of our house and studied the barn. At the far end was a corncrib with a porch that stood wagonbed high. A wide door on hand-wrought strap hinges faced a Dutch door of identical size on the back walls. There were narrow overhead rafters, and surprisingly, two windows, which probably had been louvered vents. At one time, in a short-lived venture, I used the corncrib as a small antiques shop. What it ultimately became was a crib for *storing* antiques. In good weather, I would swing the upper portion of the Dutch door open, and Jedediah, the largest of our four Labrador retrievers, would come up the steps from the back lot that spanned the length of the barn and, standing on his hindquarters, look over the door and beg to be let in. Anytime I went in the corncrib, I'd hear Jedediah clumping up the steps to the stoop. If I didn't open the top half of the door at once, he'd fuss and bark until I did. It was no wonder I had so few customers in my corncrib shop—because I put a sign out only when the mood struck me, and anyone who did come in was apt to be frightened by a large black Lab with a head the size of a bear's, woofing over the Dutch door. How were they to know the woofs were friendly and that Jeddy loved all people?

Next to the corncrib was a space enclosed by double doors that could be swung wide. This I guessed was where a buggy or carriage had been stored. The area had a dirt floor with gravel strewn about, as though someone had emptied a bucket of it. The space was about the right size for a buggy—long and not too wide. An oil-stained, wooden shelf was attached to the rear wall. I wondered if this might have been where they stored axle grease, or perhaps veterinary salves for the horses. A musty, earthy smell permeated the air, making me think that apples or potatoes had been stored there, if not grain. There was,

however, a smaller stock barn farther away from the house, so it is
likely the grain was stored there, where it would be handy for feeding
the animals in the stalls. A number of wooden brackets on the wall
indicated that saddles had been aired and kept there; there were additional pegs for bridles and other tack. It was the kind of place a child
would choose to hide when playing Hide-and-Go-Seek, with easily
opened doors and shadowy corners. The wide, open space in the middle
of the barn was paved now. Whoever spread asphalt on the circular
driveway extended the paving into the center of the barn. Where
haywagons and, later, tractors had been sheltered, we parked our station wagon and a boxy, classic Jeep wagon.

A narrow door with a long iron latch led to the stairs to the loft.
It was in that wide, spacious loft, with the broad board floor, that it
was possible to see clearly the marvelous construction of that wonderful, weathered barn. The hand-hewn roofbeam spanned the loft. Up-
rights were held in place by long pegs that shot through the joints
like wooden daggers. As the barn aged and the wood dried, the joints
became tighter and tighter. The aged wood was as hard as rock. I
believe the beams were chestnut and oak, though the question was
never positively answered.

Garden hose and irrigation equipment were stored in the loft,
but when I was in that place, I could see it piled high with hay. I
would stand in the emptiness of it, and once again I was a little girl in
the loft of the barn on our family farm in North Carolina. That barn
of my childhood was a magical place, and I loved playing in it. My
father warned me to stay out of the stalls, but in the evening, when
measures of corn and grain were poured into the troughs for the mules

and horses, I would hang on the side of a stall, watching the animals feed, and listening to the low rumbling and crunching sound as they ate. That Carolina barn had an open, central space for hay wagons or trucks. There were box stalls on each side, from front to back, except that at the end of the right side, there was a square, slatted corncrib. The corn, in papery yellow husks, was thrown in the crib in a big heap. I liked going in the crib and husking a few ears—until my hands became sore. Two sticks and a corn shuck, and I had a doll I could name and talk to. And it could be thrown away when I wished.

Horse collars and lines and feed buckets were hung on pegs in that barn. The overhead loft was the size of the barn below. There was a wide door at the front of the mow, where hay could be pitched in or out. There were no stairs to that hay loft, just a ladder nailed to the wall that led through a hole in the floor to the hay loft. I loved to go there on sunny days and watch the light slanting through the knot-holes and open spaces. Dust motes danced in those shafts of light. My cat would follow me to the barn, his route to the loft a circuitous one along beams and rafters. On rainy days I'd take a book there, and sit close by the front door of the loft, listening to the rain and reading. I'd also listen for and watch the barn mice. My cat would stalk the mice, but more often than not he'd miss them when they scurried under the hay. Long after I'd leave, Tomcat would be there, sitting quietly, staring at the hay. When fresh hay was pitched up there, and the stacks were high, I couldn't resist climbing on it. My father worried that I might fall out of the loft, and he repeatedly told me to stay down from there. But it was a special place of barn owls and barn cats, of barn mice and sweet-smelling hay. I would lie on the hay with my books, or just by myself, and dream. New hay is the itchiest stuff in Christendom, and when I came to the house, arms and legs and face red and itchy—I got a scolding for climbing in the hayloft. As I think of it, my skin begins to smart.

The loft of the old barn on Kenneth's and my "farm" in New York State was so big, I wondered if it had ever been completely filled with hay. It must have been, to have had enough to feed the stock through the long winters. I pondered one time how wonderful it would be to have a rope swing suspended from a rafter. On a rainy day, you could swing to the sound of the downpour on the tin roof. I never confessed that childlike fantasy until now. I also imagined how lovely it would be to have a flock of pigeons occupying the empty cote in the corner of the loft, where there had been pigeons before. They would have flown in the windowlike opening that framed a patch of sky. I could see the sunlight on the wings of the birds, and the patterns they would make against that square of blue sky when they tumbled through the frame. We moved before I had a chance to populate the barn with pigeons.

At the foot of the loft stairs, if you turned left and headed to the kennel in back of the barn, you would pass the barn's final appendage, a potting shed. The potting shed was built against the barn wall. Its board-and-batten construction matched that of the barn, but the barn was white, and the shed was a weathered whitewash. When I first saw the shed, it had holes in the roof, and the single door leading inside the small building hung on creaky hinges. Kenneth tinkered with the hinges and oiled them, thinking he might have to replace them. But he did not. They worked well enough. We stored pots and peat and garden tools in that shed, but it was very leaky. Fixing the roof was far down the list of things we needed to do. How it came to be repaired was bittersweet.

One winter day I was home alone when a man knocked frantically at the front door. "Call the fire department!" he yelled, wiping perspiration from his face with a handkerchief. "That big barn across the road is on fire!" Terrified for a moment that he meant *our* barn, I stepped out on the porch to see. Ours was fine, but the big barn across the highway was emitting ominous billows of smoke. I raced to the phone as he ran back toward the flaming barn. "Gotta be sure no one's in there!" he shouted. When I stepped outside, the air was heavy with smoke, and I could feel the heat. The man came over to me, and together, we silently watched fire leap through the side of the barn, then the roof. Smoke poured out of it in awful clouds. "I saw smoke and stopped," he said. "Some kids were running across the field there." He pointed to a group of houses that had been built on the farm a few years past. "I went in and called, and looked to be sure no one was still in there." "It was never used," I said. "The kids must have been playing with matches." "Smoking," he said. With a dreadful creaking and a flash of flames and sparks, the roof collapsed.

When the fire trucks came lumbering and clanging, the barn was nearly gone. It burned so fast, it was both horrifying and dazzling. I can never forget the sickening crackle and roar of that barn burning. The ferocity with which the fire consumed it was frightening. I felt immense relief that it was not *our* barn that was destroyed, but I was saddened all the same. I stood in our yard, watching the firemen across the road turn the water hoses toward our place. They sprayed water on the roof of our house in case sparks flew over and landed on it. I never thought of *that* danger! I stared at the smoldering ruin that had been a neighbor's barn, and felt the most terrible grief. It was, to me, like watching a living creature die a painful death. The ashes smoldered for days. When the smoke cleared, only the silo was left, and some twisted stanchions that stood like specters in the rubble.

Many months later, I went across the road and carefully picked my way among the burned, fallen timbers, the twisted pipes. I don't know why I went. To pay homage, perhaps. Then I noticed pressed metal shingles lying in the scorched brambles around the ruined foundation of the barn. Maybe air currents generated by the fire had blown them off the burning barn's roof—I don't know. But I started picking them up, holding them against my chest. Some were partially burned, others rusting, but I gathered a stack of those metal shingles as carefully as a prospector panning for gold. I went home with them in my arms, and put them inside the potting shed. I was sooty and my clothes filthy, but I didn't mind at all. In the weeks ahead, little by little, I worked on those precious rectangles of tin. I hammered, bent edges, scrubbed off rust with kerosene—until I thought I had enough. Then I got the ladder, a hammer, and the kind of nails the man at the hardware store had told me I'd need. The potting shed was not very tall, so it was easy to lean from the ladder and tack the recovered shingles onto the shed's roof. I put them on the way the others were placed. The pressed tin shingles were so similar to the ones already on the shed that my amateur roofing job was hardly noticeable. The roof still leaked in a heavy rain, but it was better than it had been.

Today, when I think of that old barn of ours at the corner of New Milford and Fancher Roads, in New York State, it is so good to know it is still there. I see it faded an even more delicate sienna. Stoutly pegged and beamed, it sags imperceptibly toward the creek. It is enduringly close to the land.

At the End of the Two-Mile Lane

The September day when we moved to Craig Point Farm was dry as parchment. Kenneth turned the station wagon into the rutted, dusty lane leading to the old farmhouse. The Labs, riding in back, scrambled to keep their balance. Poo, our orange tabby, carsick and miserable, crouched between us on the front seat. We wanted to get to the farm before the movers' truck arrived. I stroked the cat, trying to comfort him as we bumped toward the old white farmhouse at the lane's end. Broad fields dotted with small flocks of Canada geese stretched toward the horizon. The biblical phrase, "Fret not. Dwell in the land," flew into my thoughts like an elusive butterfly. I blinked in surprise, and it was gone. In the distance was the Choptank River glinting in the brittle autumn sunlight. On the right a tidal creek fed by the river broadened into a wide, still cove. My thoughts wandered as we approached the house. "This will be a good move for both of us. Kenneth and I can find new paths to follow." My husband was at a changing point in his career as a publisher, and I was struggling with "legal blindness," the result of surgery in which a benign tumor was removed from my optic nerve. The operation had occurred the year before. Friends said I was "handling it so well," but I knew better. I was still fighting despair and frustration.

Immediately after the operation, we lived for a year at Gibson Island, Maryland, which was convenient to Baltimore, where I went for checkups at Johns Hopkins University Hospital. At the end of the year, we needed a place to "regroup." So we set about finding a country place to lease on the Eastern Shore of Maryland. We intended to stay about six months, think things over, and enjoy a long visit in an area we both liked very much. We had spent time there at retriever trials and on weekends relaxing and enjoying the shooting trips, the picturesque Chesapeake Bay country, and the wonderful seafood.

"Here we are," Kenny said, smiling. He pulled the wagon under an apple tree. "I hope the movers don't get here for a while," he said, bailing out of the wagon like a sailor going ashore after a long tour of sea duty. He opened the back of the wagon, and the dogs jumped out. They raced in every direction. The three blacks were easier to track than Buie, the yellow; she blended with the September landscape. I took the cat in my arms. He was showing signs of recovery, lifting his head, sniffing the gentle breeze from the river. Kenneth and I were uncharacteristically quiet, absorbing the aura of peacefulness. Almost imperceptibly a feeling of calm, of hope, was edging into my consciousness, like sunlight on a gloomy day. Kenneth broke the spell. As he was searching for the house keys in his pocket, he whistled for the dogs. "Wonder how old those trees are?" Tall black walnut and sycamore trees shaded the parking space. Peering upward, squinting, I said, "Can't guess. Do I see lots of walnuts?" Swinging the key on his finger, he ruefully studied the plentiful crop. "They're hell to shell. Green ones stain your hands, dry ones tear 'em up."

"There's a chestnut tree, too," I said pointing. "We can have chestnut stuffing for Thanksgiving."

"Chestnut and *oyster* stuffing," he corrected. "Come on, we're planning holidays before we've seen the house again." Still holding Poo in my arms, I followed Kenneth toward the kitchen door.

"Look! I'd forgotten there were magnolias. I love magnolias."

"You would," he laughed. "Come on, Scarlett." At the back step, I touched his arm. "Just a minute," I said. "Smell the river?" He nodded. Now I was ready for all the decisions about where to place the furniture, and where the boxes should go.

Craig Point, as the name suggests, is a peninsula. Behind the house, fields reached to the Choptank river. In front, from the cove, Reed's Creek curved around the land to meet the Choptank. The farm-

house, built in the 1700s, had simple architectural grace. It stood with its back to the prevailing wind and faced the creek, cove, and landing. Neatly trimmed beds of ivy hugged the foundation of the house. Beside a small front porch were deep-green, mature boxwoods.

Kenneth unlocked the door and we stepped into the kitchen. It was, we soon learned, where everyone came in. No one ever walked around to the front door. The kitchen door still had a wrought-iron handle and thumb latch.

The Labs followed us, their footsteps echoing hollowly in the empty rooms. I bent over and dropped the cat on the floor. Poo leaped to a countertop and settled near a window. It became his favorite spot in the kitchen. From that cozy roost, he could watch birds, and he was first to see who was coming down the lane.

The square kitchen most likely was the first room built. "Telescope" houses, in which rooms were added to the original part of the house like the sections of a telescope, were common on the Eastern Shore, where acreage was no problem. Usually, each addition was stepped up from and wider than the last. If such a house could be tipped on one end, the rooms would collapse into one another in the manner of a telescope. If someone stood in the kitchen at Craig Point, and looked through the aligned doors of the other rooms, he could see to the other end of the house. I sometimes wondered if any children with peashooters ever had tried to reach from the kitchen to the other end. The question remains unsolved. As the planter's family and needs grew, he added rooms, possibly even a second story.

I felt at home at Craig Point immediately, as though it was familiar territory. It was comfortable, and had an aura of life continuing. So strong was my sense of familiarity to the kitchen, I had a sudden and profound sense of peace. When the movers arrived, we put my parents' round oak table in front of the fireplace in the kitchen. It looked as though it had always been there. We tucked our plank seat chairs around it. We angled two easy chairs beside the fireplace. In the fireplace was the original iron bracket and hook that was to hold a cook pot over the coals. I imagined (had a sense of *knowing*) the simple joy of another woman, at another time, stirring a clove-scented pot of fox-grape jam over the fire. ("What an imagination!" my mother always said—without discouraging it.) But an interesting thing happened some time afterward when our nephew visited us. After a walk down to the river, he came into the kitchen—carrying a hat full of fox grapes he had picked. Fox grapes are small, and removing the seed is tedious. We made fox-grape jam, though, and sealed it in small jars. That kitchen, with its pine cupboards and a window facing the river, must always have been a cozy place. I guessed there had been a long rifle over the fireplace and a powder horn hanging from the plain mantle. The housewife in the kitchen could gaze out the window and see her husband walking up from the river, very possibly with a brace of ducks in hand. Many a duck and goose had been cooked in that kitchen. The feathers and down would have been used to stuff pillows and feather ticks. The room was full of memories. During our tenancy, it continued to be a busy room. Everyone hung around in the kitchen.

"Come in here," Kenneth called from the living room, his voice stirring me out of my mental meandering. "We need to decide where to put the highboy. Can't have the movers holding it in midair while we make up our minds." I hurried toward the door leading to the dining room. Suddenly, I bumped into something, stumbled, and fell flat on my face. I sat up, face flushed, heart thumping, feeling foolish. I rubbed my scraped elbow, surprised to feel tears slipping down my cheeks.

"Damn!" I huffed. "Dammit it anyway!"

Kenneth was there instantly. My six-foot body had hit the floor with a mighty thump. "Are you hurt?" He leaned down to help me up.

"Only my dignity. I jarred my parts and bruised my shins." He helped me to my feet. I dusted my clothes and grinned sheepishly. "I'll have to remember that step when I'm bringing hot soup to the dining room," I said, walking warily in his direction. We both laughed.

"Watch that step up into the living room!" Kenneth warned. "Come look out here, Jo."

He had the front door open. I stepped around the dogs. They were sprawled on the bare floor, snoozing, very much at home. Out on the front porch were two Dutch-style benches. The distinctive smell of boxwood and the scent of the distant river filled the air. Left of the porch, a thick spruce towered high above the roofline. We learned, in time, that it was a nesting place for mourning doves.

Wide lawn swept from house to creek. Two old pear trees bent away from fields and the river. We would fill many baskets with pears from those gnarled trees. On the opposite side of the lawn, a thicket of wild cherry, scrub oak and Osage orange, and tangled honeysuckle separated the yard from a narrow dirt road that led to the landing. The thicket also shielded the view of a well-established asparagus patch and vegetable garden behind the caretaker's cottage.

The lawn was cut short from the house halfway to the creek. At midpoint it gave way to a knee-high meadow of grass, weeds, and wildflowers. The meadow ended at the brushy, reedy shoreline, where red-winged blackbirds were singing their wheezy song.

A narrow dock on slender pilings threaded into Reed's Creek. The tide was in. A crab boat and a couple of other small craft rode high at their moorings on the glassy water. At the head of the pier was a shed where crab pots, bushel baskets, and fish nets were stored. Close by the shed was a weathered dinghy upturned on sawhorses. Milkweed and pokeweed grew out from under the dinghy, where no mower could reach.

In the old days visitors came by boat. "There must have been a clear path from the dock to the house," I said. "Because no lady in a long dress could make it through those weeds without exposing her pantaloons!"

"You're hopeless," Kenneth laughed. "Let's go upstairs and see where we want to put the beds."

We went up the steep stairs. The steps were so narrow it was easier if we placed our feet sideways. The bedroom at the head of the stairs had dormer windows with a view of creek and river. Down the hall was a very small room with a single window and a fireplace. "Must have been the nursery," Kenneth said. (It became my hideaway.) Next there was a bath. At the end of the hall, down two steep steps, was a large, sunny bedroom. A door lead to a walk-in attic in which there were clothes racks. We soon knew why. The bedroom closet was rather cramped, but some houseguests were reluctant to use the attic storage space. Many said it was "spooky." It did not help when I told them "only friendly ghosts stay here."

That September day when we moved to Craig Point Farm lingers warmly in my mind. I remember the wonderful, open space of the unfurnished house, like an empty ballroom, and my giddy urge to dance. Soon the space had piled high with boxes and furniture. The day was exhausting and exhilarating. That night, bone weary and happy in our downstairs bedroom, we had pushed unpacked cartons aside and fallen into bed.

Next morning, just before dawn, when the sky turned rosy and the sun was breaking through, there came a sound from the creek that I will never forget. First, faint gabbling. Then the splendid sound of a flock of wild geese lifting off the creek, and rising higher and higher in the sky. They flew away to feed in the fields. We listened quietly. We lay there, not wishing to break the spell. And once more, that elusive phrase crept into my consciousness: "Dwell in the land."

DAY OF REST

Stubbly and dusted with snow
the cornfield is dotted with geese.
Like stout little men
with their hands in their pockets,
The white-vested Canadas lean back,
Stroll and take the winter sun.
Gabbling drowsily across the rows,
Safe from the hunter's gun,
They seem to know
It's Sunday.

The Healing Land

Spending time alone and relating to the natural world are a powerful combination when someone is looking for an answer, searching for a way of going. I didn't really know I was searching for anything. I was living day to day a life that had changed dramatically. I had plenty of time alone to deal with it.

I knew perfectly well that I had zero depth perception, but I persisted in walking only with a short cane. It was too short to tell me the depth of a step, or help me anticipate an incline or decline. So I was physically off balance as well as stubborn. After a certain number of tumbles, however, even the most resistant person begins to have a glimmer of understanding that things are going to be different now, whether you like it or not. Finally, I rang up the Department of Blind Services and was told that mobility training was available at Salisbury, Maryland, only an hour away from Craig Point. I was waiting for Kenneth when he came home that night.

"I've made an appointment for a mobility lesson in Salisbury. Will you drive me there? I'll have to go for a series of sessions."

"Of course I will. It's a great idea." He didn't add that it was high time.

At the first session, the instructor, who was steadily going blind himself from macular degeneration, said, "How're you doing?"

"OK," I lied.

"Not with that cane, you're not," he said, leveling a gaze on me that I knew was blurred. I had the feeling he knew what I was feeling, and more.

"Good grief, woman!" he exploded. "You're going to get yourself killed with that stupid cane. Come here."

I went to the corner he indicated. He selected a long, white cane from a cluster of canes in the corner.

"This should be just right. It should reach from the floor to your shoulder." He stood the cane next to my tense body, measuring.

"That's it," he said. "Take it."

I took the cane with the reluctance of someone who has been commanded to grasp a hot poker. The white cane was symbolic of everything I was resisting, denying. But I took it. The mobility training involved being blindfolded so that I wouldn't rely on my low vision for getting around. I was trained to get around in total darkness, like someone totally blind. I was taught to swing the cane from side to side in front of me as I walked. The instructor showed me how to estimate the size of a place by tapping the floor or wall and listening to the sound. He taught me to count doors in a long hall in order to find the one I wanted, how to go up and down stairs, cross a busy street, make my way along a crowded sidewalk, board a bus, find my way back to where I started. In the beginning, I was nervous, but as I practiced, I relaxed. Taking mobility training was the most important step in accepting my visual problem. Being with others who were totally blind jolted me into understanding how prideful

I had been, and how lucky I was that I had even the slightest bit of vision. I had known this all along, but my sorrow at being changed from a very active, independent person to one who no longer could do some of the things I loved—and one who had to ask for help, and a ride—was hard to overcome.

Before I had mobility training, I was careful not to go far from the house, because I could easily become disoriented and have trouble finding my way back to the house. So after I had tended to the chores that I could tend to inside, if the weather was nice, I'd sit on the front steps and think and be still. The sun felt so good, and it made me feel better. I could smell the creek, hear small birds fluttering in and out of the boxwoods. Sometimes I caught a glimpse of one. Tar would stay with me. If I said, "Go ahead," he'd trot off toward the creek, or down to the thicket. He'd come when I called or whistled. When I patted him, his coat was warm from the sun. Something as simple as sitting in the sun and tuning in to the world around me made me feel better.

Using my cane and my new skills, I could now walk freely around the grounds, being careful to count my steps, or using something that I could see, like the front porch or the apple tree, as a landmark. Walking down the lawn, through the meadow grass, and to the dock at the creek was an easy, straight shot. Tar trotted along. I found that I could safely make my way along the narrow dock. The end of the dock became one of my favorite places for contemplation. I'd sit there and listen to the water, feel the breeze from the river, and listen to the birds. I could hear boats out on the river. In time, I was able to walk along the single board that stretched from the dock to a piling out in the creek. Our boat swung at anchor there. After a while, I had no trouble boarding the boat from that single board. The summer day that I summoned the courage to walk to the river at the point, I felt like an explorer. It was only about a mile, maybe a mile and a half to the river, but it seemed like the end of the earth to me. I decided to take all four dogs with me. I put on my straw hat, and we set out. I tapped along one side of the lane. The track that I followed was hard packed and dry, and thumped hollowly as I tapped along it. The dogs ran through the fields bordering the road, galloping back to me now and again, to see if I was coming. A trip that took a few minutes by car seemed to take a long time by foot. But I really didn't have any trouble. When I heard the Labs splashing in water, I knew I was close. I passed the marsh on the right that we had to cross to get to the beach on the creek. I kept going, and suddenly, I could hear water sloshing on the shore of the point. I had reached the river. Christopher Columbus could not have been more excited when he made landfall than when I found the Choptank River. It gave me an incredible sense of new freedom. The dogs explored the shoreline, plunged in the cool water. I waded in the shallow water, then sat on shore a while. Then the three black Labs, the yellow Lab, and I started our journey home. I was glad for the first sight of the old farmhouse, and the dogs were panting and thirsty after their run. With the hose, I filled their buckets with fresh water. I went into the kitchen for a glass of iced tea. I felt my old self-confidence.

Being often alone on the farm, I realized that the very land, water, and sky helped me to regain my perspective and sense of well-being. It was clear to me that what we have is more important than what we have not. It was then I began to write again.

A Sense of Place

At Craig Point we lived by the seasons, anticipating the quality and natural events like the lyrics of a familiar song. Time actually had a lyrical, flowing quality. Perhaps it was being on that point, so open and subject to the elements, or perhaps it was the proximity of land and water that brought seasonal phenomena that we accepted and absorbed. I felt an easy and natural flow of time there that I had not experienced since childhood.

Before spring arrived, you could smell it coming, as the last traces of snow melted and the soggy fields warmed and dried under intensifying sun and quickening breeze. Farmers would stride across the fields, stopping to feel the soil, lifting a handful where it was drying, to feel it, smell it, and estimate when planting could begin. After hard spring rains, we'd get calls from people who wanted to search the fields for Indian artifacts, for it was believed that Pokomoke Indians had lived along the river and on Craig Point. Visitors often found arrowheads and other bits and pieces of stone that might have been part of an ancient tool. Wild cress appeared in the fields and dandelions polka dotted the long stretch of lawn leading to Reed's Creek, behind the house. Birds were busy nesting in the boxwoods beside the house, and in honeysuckle and thicket. Mourning doves nested in the tall spruce near our bedroom window. The last geese had flown off to nesting grounds in the Arctic, and once again the soft sounds of sparrows and songbirds were clear in the air. Each morning and evening the mockingbird perched on the peak of the wellhouse, and sang his splendid song. At water's edge, red-winged blackbirds sang, and a few mallards that stayed year round blasted the silence with their noisy quacking. And over the slowly drying fields, the crows tumbled and soared, jet-black feathers flashing iridescent in the sun. Their merry cawing helped to fill the silence. I could hear the chink-chink of mooring lines against metal, as boats at the dock rode the rising tide in Reed's Creek. The air was fragrant with the smell of loam, tender grass, clover, spring flowers, and the tang of the sea. Down the lane the fisherman spread his nets to dry

near the apple tree that was a blur of pinkish-white blossoms. He stacked his bushel baskets, ready to tote tomorrow's catch to market. With the nets billowing slightly in the breeze, he walked away down the side lane to cut a mess of asparagus in his garden. His chunky Lab trotted alongside.

In spring the clothesline in the side yard was heavy with quilts that had been washed and hung to dry before they were stored until fall. As the wind from the river steadily dried them, they lightened in weight, and flapped smartly. Sheets drying on the line in a high wind would sometimes crack like rifle shot. Our dogs would roll and roll in the new grass, and slosh in the creek when we walked out on the creaky, narrow dock. We opened windows and doors, cleaned closets, waxed floors, and put away winter clothes and eliminated the clutter in the house that made it seem cozy in winter, but was oppressive in summer. We cleaned the porch, repaired screens, painted wicker, and planted a small vegetable garden and flowers. Spring came jubilantly and unmistakably to Craig Point—as bright and sweet as strawberries.

Summer crept up and landed with a blast of heat. One minute the corn and soybeans were growing, the tomatoes were green, days were warm and nights were cool—and the next, crops were vigorously maturing, tomatoes ripened, and the first armload of Silver Queen corn was tossed on the picnic table near the kitchen door. And the temperature skyrocketed. In summer, furious squalls would roll in off the river, crashing and flashing. The rain was torrential and brief. In a matter of minutes, the squall would end and the sky would clear. The whole world seemed fresh and green after such a storm, and the after-rain smell of the country was sweet and indescribable. Often, after these squalls, we would see spectacular, luminous rainbows bridging the sky. Summers at Craig Point could deepen into the torrid heat of the tropics. Plaster walls in the old farmhouse would sweat and sometimes mildew. When we were outside in the sun, our clothes clung to our bodies like damp rags, and moisture fairly hung in the air. The land was lush, and the wind from the river was hot. At such times, we found relief from the heat by picnicking on the little sandy crescent beach at the mouth of Reed's Creek. At the tip of the point, the shape of the beach changed from year to year, depending on the violence of the current where the creek met the Choptank River. We could walk down the farm lane leading to the river, or take the boat from the dock down to the beach. It was the favorite picnic spot of our friends on the Fourth of July. After the first Independence Day picnic there, they didn't ask *if* we were having the picnic, they just asked what time they should come, and what they should bring. Some events take on a life of their own, and become a tradition. When we went to the beach, we'd anchor the boat in shallow water and wade ashore with beach umbrellas and other gear. If we walked, we'd make our way through a reedy marsh to get to the sand. We could swim there, and it was not uncommon to see all the picnickers standing neck deep in the water, trying to stay cool. We had an inflated tractor tube that was perfect for lounging and playing in the water. Towed on a long line behind the boat, it gave anyone willing to try it a bumpy ride. We always stayed in the creek when towing the tube, so that if it should come loose, anyone aboard it could easily float ashore.

When it was a dry summer, the lane to the highway was like corrugated metal. Windblown dust from the fields meant endless dusting in the house, and discomfort outside. On these hot, dry days heat shimmered over the land like quivering light.

But when gentle breezes and rain from the direction of the river balanced with summer heat, it was wonderful on the point. It was the

time of crab feasts, when we would steam the blue claws by the bushel.
We'd put our order for crabs in with our waterman neighbor the day
before we wanted them. Early on a summer morning, I'd hear Earl
putt-putting out the creek in his boat. He would be on his way to his
favorite places to crab. His boat was rigged with a roller at the stern,
over which the crab line, baited at intervals, could be let out and
spooled in. He had affixed a long tiller to the outboard motor. When
the baited line was all in the water, he'd swing the boat around, stand
amidships, and steer with his foot on the long tiller while he started
back down the crab line. With a long-handled net, he'd dip crabs that
clung to the baited line, as the line was slowly pulled to the surface of
the water, and then aboard. It was a tricky business—keeping the
boat going in the right direction, and deftly swooping the crabs up
and dumping them in a basket quickly, before another crab surfaced.
After each run, bait had to be checked, and the line let out again.
Some days he caught only a few, sometimes more than he could sell at
the local fish markets. On such occasions, he'd give us free crabs, or
sell us choice, fat "jimmies" for a very low price.

Picking crabmeat from a steamed crab is tediously slow for many,
and quick as lightning for professional "pickers." Sometimes, if we
knew we were having company, Anna (my friend and helper) and I
would pick a mess of crabs so we could have crabcakes when the guests
arrived. If you ever do this one time, you will understand why the
price of crabmeat stays high. It is the custom in Maryland, when
having a crab feast, to steam the crabs, and when they're done—dump
them out on a table covered with several thicknesses of newspapers.
Small wooden hammers, picks, and plierslike crackers are handed out,

and then it's each feaster for himself. Even after getting the hang of picking the meat from a steamed crab, it takes a lot of work to satisfy one's appetite. But when the bright-red crabs, redolent of "Old Bay" seasoning, are piled on the table, still steaming, there are few who do not hasten to join the feast. Especially when there are corn on the cob and cold beer as accompaniments.

There were times, in summer, when heavy thunderclouds slid in from the Chesapeake almost daily, and the rain went on for days. Storms on the point, at any time of year, were spectacular. But summer was mostly lazy and slower paced, when the fishing villages were filled with tourists and boat people who were sailing the Chesapeake Bay waters. Summer evenings at Craig Point were traced with honeysuckle, freshly cut grass, and river breeze. Before the mosquitoes came whining at dark, twinkling clouds of fireflies would lift from the lawn and drift skyward in the gathering dark. We'd sit on the screen porch, watching them.

Fall came subtly, in quick bursts of cool air, and in the crunch of drying grass underfoot. River water and creek water both lost some of their murkiness when cooler weather came. The fields would be thick with milkweed, drying grasses, faded Queen Anne's lace, and rattly seed pods. Combines in the fields, harvesting soybeans and corn, created miniature dust storms behind them. Pumpkins and colorful squashes and red and yellow corn were in the roadside stands, and the spicy scent of chrysanthemum filled rooms where the flowers stood in shaggy jewel-toned bouquets. When only bean and corn stubble was left in the field, the landscape, almost imperceptibly, faded to amber, then tones of beige and brown—like a monochromatic painting. The river glinted blue in the autumn light.

In the mornings, the air became crisp and tart as apple cider, and trees showed brilliant red, russet, yellow, and orange. We quickened our steps, and walks along the lanes were once again pleasant. The staccato of walnuts and chestnuts and Osage oranges falling to the ground was counterpointed by the constant whir of locusts. We replenished the woodpile, and one evening it would be cool enough for the first fire. And then one morning, most likely when we were having coffee, we'd hear it: the faint cry of high-flying geese. It was always exciting! It was generally in mid-September when we heard the first flight of geese coming back to their winter feeding grounds at Craig Point. We never could stay inside when we heard the geese. We'd hurry out and watch the sky. The sound of the flying birds would be faint, then grow closer and louder, and before long we'd spot the first V, as they circled the farm, honking. Even as I think of it today, it lifts my heart and takes my breath. It is one of nature's most splendid symbols of the changing seasons. The great, gray, mag-

nificent Canadas would whiffle on the wind, and tumble into the golden fields.

By the time the migration was complete, thousands of Canada geese would be on the Eastern Shore, and many, many flocks fed and rested in the fields at Craig Point. The sound of their gabbling was wonderful to hear. And when they lifted off to fly away, their honking was remarkable. The Canadas were our magnificent neighbors all fall and winter. In my mind, the sound of the geese is mixed with the smell of ripening apples and wood smoke in the air. I never tired of hearing them, and whenever things were stressful, pausing to listen to the geese always relieved tension. Our Labrador retrievers were more lively and invigorated when autumn weather arrived, but after a few dashes toward nearby flocks of geese while we whistled and scolded, they soon ignored the flocks. And the geese paid no attention to the Labs. It was as though they checked one another out, and it was understood that there was to be a peaceable arrangement. When the leaves drifted down, and the wind swept them into deep swirls and waves, and the nights grew colder, autumn had taken hold. Through the bare branches of the trees, riding high in the sky, was the wolf moon, the hunter's moon.

Autumn's slipping into winter was gradual, hardly noticeable until the frost became more frequent, and suddenly the temperature dropped, and the wind from the river was breathtakingly cold. Wind would howl around the house, whining at the chimneys. Snow never seemed to drift gently on Craig Point, but rather came in windy spirals and wisps, like tattered lace curtains floating on the wind. Light snowfalls dusted the corn stubble with white, coated the roof, and decorated the shrubs. Heavy snowstorms and blizzards on the point were fierce and blinding. The snow piled deep along the river, in the fields, and around the house. It buried the woodpile and filled the kennel runs. We'd have to dig out the kitchen door, dig a path to the woodpile and another to the station wagon, and dig out the kennels. If the temperature dropped below a certain level, we always brought all the dogs inside. Their houses were designed to withstand the cold, but when the wind was added to the snow and dropping temperature, it was unbearable. Besides, we liked having the dogs inside, and they loved sprawling in front of the fire. So did Poo, the cat.

Once after a storm when the temperature dropped precipitously, and the wind roared incessantly against the house, we awakened to a snowbound land's shining light, with the frozen river in the distance. When Kenneth got around to digging out the kennels, he found many small, frozen birds that had taken refuge from the wind in the dog-houses—a bitter, poignant reminder of the power of the elements. When the two-mile lane was deep in snow, we were totally snow-bound. We had to wait to be plowed out. Other than by helicopter, or a long, hard trek through heavy drifts, there was no way out. When snow finally began to melt, it was a challenge to make it in or out on that slippery lane. Christmas in that old Maryland farmhouse was cozy and beautiful. With boxwood, holly, and magnolia trees, there was plenty of greenery for decorating. Family and friends always congregated in the warm kitchen and by the living-room fire. In both fall and winter, oysters from the Choptank and other Chesapeake estuaries were plump, salty, and highly prized by oyster-lovers. We had them on the half shell, steamed, "Rockefellered," scalloped, stewed, frittered, and fried. They were wonderful, and always a favorite with houseguests. And oyster stuffing was just right for a holiday bird. Living close to the oyster beds of local waters provided a succulent reminder of a special season.

Dull gray days of winter were enlivened by flocks of ducks and geese flying over the frozen river, and by the constant movement of the Canadas in and out of the fields and creek. There was a special warmth to that old house in winter, and it helped the coldest season along. We went away to the Caribbean a few times, and as much as I love warm weather, the farmhouse was a happy sight when we returned. We'd always drop our suitcases in the kitchen, and hurry to build a fire in the fireplace in the living room. Firelight and candlelight were appropriate at the old house.

Finally, the winds would slacken, the ice in the river would break up and melt, and one day that loamy smell of spring coming up from the South would be in the air. Almost before we knew it, flood tides would lift the moored boats almost as high as the dock, and we would see our neighbor inspecting his boat. We'd walk to the beach, still in heavy sweaters, to see if there was much damage at the water's edge and come home to warm ourselves beside a gentle fire. As the sun warmed the earth and the first daffodil appeared, there suddenly would be a great silence in the land. While we slept, the geese had flown away in the moonlight. Then we knew for certain that spring was here again.

Living in the natural pattern of the seasons, close to the land, water, and sky—quite simply, helped me to get well, to renew my optimism and perspective. When we are ill, grieving, tired, or dispirited, we long to be in beautiful, natural places—by the sea, in the hills or desert, by still waters, wherever we can find blue sky, trees, flowers, meadows, birdsong. Where there is peace and quiet. I cannot imagine who would long for pavement, grime, traffic, noise, concrete. Being aware of the splendor of the seasons, of the natural world, makes us understand man's critical need for wild places. Living with familiar things and moving in the seasons can fulfill that profound need common to us all: a sense of place.

DATE DUE		
JUL 2 2 1995		
APR 1 7 1997		
AUG 1 5 2000		